CALIFORNIA
REAL ESTATE PRINCIPLES
WORKBOOK

Second Edition

Real Estate Salesperson
and Broker License
Exam Preparation

California Real Estate Principles Workbook, Second Edition

ISBN 1419505475

PPN 6401-7807

Published by Anthony Schools®, A Kaplan Professional Company.

© 2004 DF Institute, Inc.

Disclaimer

This material is for educational purposes only. In no way should any statements or summaries be used as a substitute for legal or tax advice.

10 9 8 7

Printed in the United States

Introduction

KEYS TO SUCCESS

Welcome to *Anthony Schools'* California Real Estate Principles program!

Congratulations, you are on the road to a new career. If you have been away from an academic environment for some time there is no need to worry. We will guide you to success.

You have selected our Home Study Real Estate Principles program that we supplement with optional LIVE classroom sessions. You will discover that these live sessions provide an invaluable opportunity to further enhance your learning through the guidance of a real estate expert. Upon completion of this program, you will have met all of the education requirements to be eligible to take the California State Salesperson License Examination.

Included in the materials you received are:

- *California Real Estate Principles* textbook, by Stapleton and Williams. That book presents the subject matter you are expected to learn.

- *California Real Estate Principles Workbook,* which will be the book used in class. It gives you an opportunity to interact with the material and provides additional examples to enhance your learning and broaden your understanding.

- *California Real Estate Power Test Program,* which provides sample questions, answers, and explanations.

Important: Read the instructions on next page.

Steps for Ensuring Your Success

1. Apply **IMMEDIATELY** to the Department of Real Estate for your state examination date (if you haven't already done so). You will be scheduled to take your exam in approximately eight to ten weeks from the date that you send in your application.

2. As soon as you submit your application for your state exam, call our Customer Service office at **888-419-9599** to reserve a seat for our Exam Prep Review. You should attend this Review one to three weeks before your state exam date.

3. At home, before class, preview the reading assignments in your textbook that are going to be covered in class.

   Please attend all of your scheduled classes. It is preferable, but certainly not necessary to take them in the order of the Workbook. It is always possible to make up a missed session. However, it is best to complete the entire program in as short a time as possible. Do not drag it out, because you will begin to forget much of the important material you learned at the beginning.

   Always bring your *Workbook* to class. Take notes directly in your *Workbook* and use a highlighter. Always feel free to ask your instructor about material that is not clear to you. It is not necessary to bring your textbook to class; but read it at home.

4. After class, review the material in this Workbook that was covered in class and do the Glossary Review and Review Exam at the end of each Unit.

5. After 18 days have passed from the date you registered for this course, you can take the "open book" final examination for this *California Real Estate Principles* course. Upon passing, you will receive a completion Certificate.

6. While you are waiting for your state exam test date, work with your *California Real Estate Power Test Program*. Follow the directions that are included. There is no better preparation during this time than working with practice questions.

7. Attend your Two-Day Exam Prep Review! Please bring a calculator. All other materials will be provided.

Here's to your success!

Ted Highland
Director of Education

Acknowledgements

We at Anthony Schools are grateful for all of our staff and instructors whose contributions and enthusiasm made this work possible. We would like to especially thank the following for their valuable assistance:

- Steve Crane
- Edna Deeb
- Linda Galluccio
- Gary King
- Rick Larson
- Steve Oxman
- Jeff Parsons
- Ann Rankin
- Heather Staudinger
- Jim Tack
- Bobra Tahan
- Alan Tochterman
- Art Valenzuela
- Jason Wolins
- Susan Wooten

They have been extremely generous with their time and expertise in producing an up-to-date and attractive resource for our students and customers.

Thank you for your fine work.

Table of Contents

Unit 4: Real Estate Contracts/Subdivision Law, continued

Unit 5: Finance, continued

Unit 6: Appraisal.. 107

Unit 1: The Nature, Description, and Use of Real Estate

Lecture Outline and Notes

Key topics in this unit:

- The difference between real estate and personal property
- The three legal methods of land description
- How government rights affect ownership
- How the government controls land use

Reading assignments (in <u>California Real Estate Principles, 6th Edition</u> textbook)

- Chapter 1: The Nature of Real Property
- Chapter 2: Land Use Regulations

I.   **REAL ESTATE / REAL PROPERTY**

Includes land plus improvements, rights, appurtenances, and fixtures

     A.   **Land**

          1.

          2.

          3.

     B.   **Improvements**

          1.   Items affixed to the land with the intent of being permanent

          2.   Examples:

     C.   **Rights**

          1.   Air rights

                 •

                 •

2.   Water Rights – Right of Reasonable Usage

    a.   Riparian rights

-

        •   If water is navigable, land owned to high-water line

        •   If not navigable, land owned to center of waterway

    b.   Littoral rights

-

    c.   Land can be lost or gained through the action of water:

        •   Sudden loss of land through natural causes:

        •   Gradual loss of land through natural causes:

        •   Addition to land through natural forces:

        •   Taking title to additional property through accretion or attachment:

3.   Mineral Rights

D.   Appurtenances

1.   Something that goes with ("runs with") the land

2.   Example - stock in a mutual water company cannot be sold separately and is considered real property

II.   PERSONAL PROPERTY (CHATTEL)

A.

B.   Movable items

C.   Example: Mobile homes are personal property unless permanently attached to a foundation.

III.   LAW OF FIXTURES

    A.   Fixture Defined

    An item of personal property that is attached to the land in such a manner as to be considered part of the real property

    B.   Tests of a fixture:

    1.   Agreement

    2.   Intent – was the object affixed or installed with the intent of improving the land?

    3.   Relationship of the parties to the object –

    4.   Adaptation
    Garage door openers, house keys are considered fixtures.

    5.   Method of Attachment

    C.   Exceptions

    1.   Trade Fixtures: Tenant-installed additions that are a necessary part of the tenant's trade or business. Tenant may remove trade fixtures prior to lease termination. Tenant is responsible for any damage caused by removal. If not removed, they belong to the landlord (through accession).

    2.   Emblements: Annually cultivated crops that belong to a tenant who planted them unless otherwise agreed.

IV. LEGAL METHODS OF LAND DESCRIPTION

Metes and Bounds; Rectangular (Government) Survey; Lot and Block

A. Metes and Bounds

1. "Metes" means measures in feet, inches, etc. "Bounds" means shape or boundaries.

2.

3. Completely encircle property with description.

4. Complex method;

Example -

A tract of land located in the Village of Red Skull, described as follows: Beginning at the intersection of the East line of Jones Road and the South line of Skull Drive; thence East along the South line of Skull Drive 200 feet; thence South 15° East 216.5 feet, more or less, to the center thread of Red Skull Creek; thence Northwesterly along the center line of said Creek to its intersection with the East line of Jones Road; thence North 105 feet, more or less, along the East line of Jones Road to the place of beginning.

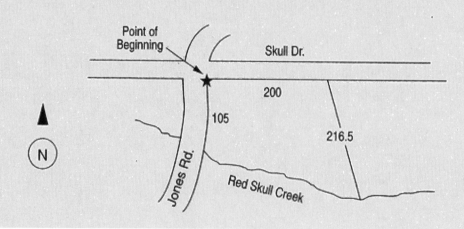

B.   **U.S. Government (Rectangular) Survey**

Primarily used for large parcels of rural property.

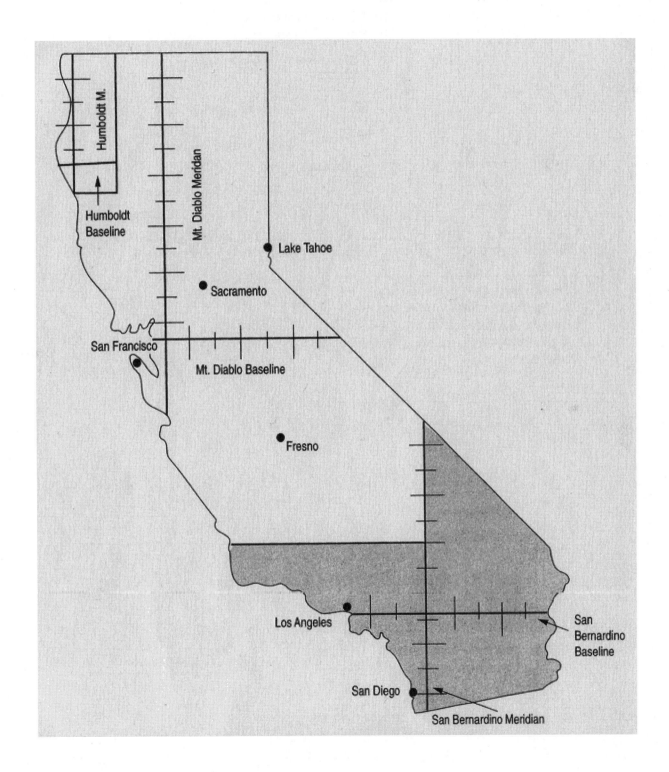

U.S. Government (Rectangular) Survey Example

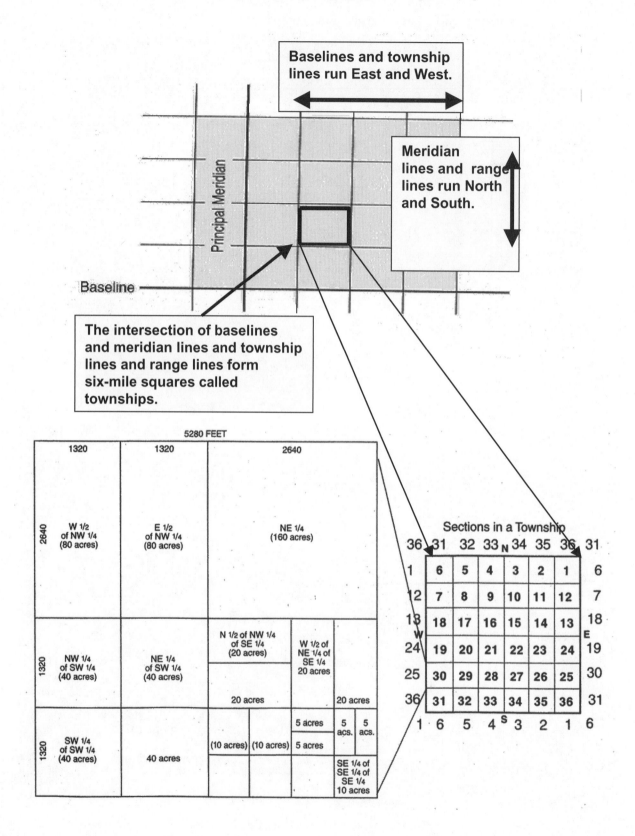

UNITS OF MEASUREMENT

- Townships are six miles square.

- Townships contain 36 square miles.

- One township contains 36 sections, numbered from the northeast (NE) corner (as shown on the previous page).

- Sections are one mile square.

- One mile is 5,280 lineal feet.

- One section contains 640 acres.

- One acre contains 43,560 square feet.

- One yard equals three feet.

Example of Computing Land Area

How many acres are in the E ½ of the NE ¼ of the NW ¼ of Section 1?

C. Lot and Block System

Also known as the "lot, block, and tract system," the "subdivision system," or the "recorded plat." Primarily used for urban residential property.

1.   Plat or subdivision map = Map showing location and boundaries of individual lots in a land subdivision, drawn to scale. The plat is recorded in the county recorder's office of the county in which the property is located.

2.   Contains **contiguous lots**, meaning lots that touch at any point including a corner.

Example –

In the following diagram, what lots are contiguous to Lot 6?

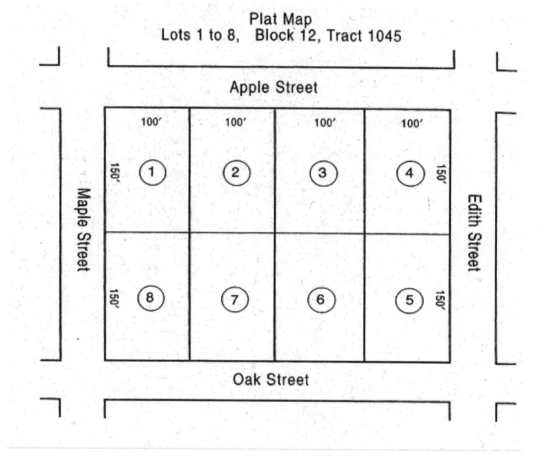

V.   GOVERNMENTAL RIGHTS IN LAND
(Memory aid is **P-E-T-E**)

A.   Police Power

　　1.

　　2.   Zoning, planning, building codes (codes to enhance public safety)

　　3.   Not considered "taking" therefore property owner is not due compensation

B.   Eminent Domain

　　1.

　　2.

　　3.   Compensation (value plus "damages")

　　4.   "Inverse condemnation" is an owner-initiated court action seeking compensation from the government when the owner's property has been substantially interfered with by governmental action.

C.   Taxes and Special Assessments

　　1.

　　2.

　　3.   are taxes levied against specific properties that benefit from a public improvement.

　　4.   Mello-Roos Act of 1982 allowed for another type of assessment that doesn't have to benefit individual properties. Billed separately from property taxes. Lien must be disclosed by seller of a 1-to-4 unit dwelling.

D.   Escheat

　　1.

　　2.   Exercised when owner dies intestate (no will) and without heirs

VI. GOVERNMENT LAND USE CONTROLS

Authority is derived from government's police power

A. Master (General) Development Plan

1. Land survey showing present and future use of properties

2. Economic survey showing present and future economic base of the area

B. Land Use Zone Classifications:

Residential

-

-

Commercial

Industrial/Manufacturing

Agricultural

Mixed

Public

Note: A **buffer zone** is an area of land that separates two drastically different land use zones.

C. Land Use Restrictions

1. Purpose is to protect against uncontrolled growth, protect public health, and preserve compatibility.

2. Setback/Sideyard/Rearyard restrictions specify the location of improvements in relation to boundaries.

Orientation:

3. Minimum frontage requirements specify acceptable building sites.

D.   Building Codes

1.   Designed to provide minimum construction standards

2.   Permits and inspections provide evidence of compliance.
       Building inspectors   – can grant

3.   Federal and local standards may conflict.

E.   Zoning Changes/Deviations

1.   Amendment is a zoning change for an entire area.

2.   Nonconforming use allows owner to continue present use that no longer complies
       with current zoning.

       i.   Sometimes called

       ii.   May not

3.   Variance allows individual owner to vary or deviate from strict compliance with
       zoning in order to relieve or prevent economic hardship.

4.   Conditional use is a specific type of variance allowing a different use.
       Owner obtains a

5.   "Downzoning" is a zoning change from dense to less dense usage.

6.   "Spot zoning" is a reclassification of a small area of land for use that does not
       conform to the surroundings.

Unit 1: Glossary Review

fixture	variance
grandfather clause	subdivision plat
avulsion	building codes
riparian	R3
littoral	downzoning
accession	

1. Building inspectors are primarily liable for the enforcement of _____.

2. The zoning code for multifamily dwellings is _____.

3. A _____ allows a property owner to deviate from zoning requirements.

4. A change in zoning from more dense to less dense use (for example, commercial to residential) is called _____.

5. _____ rights deal with streams, river, and watercourses.

6. _____ rights deal with lakes and oceans.

7. _____ is taking title to additional property through accretion or attachment.

8. _____ is a sudden and perceptible loss of land by the action of water as by a sudden change in the course of a river.

9. A_____ allows for non-conforming use when zoning changes.

10. A plan showing the lot dimensions and boundaries and drawn to scale is called a _____.

11. An item of personal property that has been permanently affixed to real property so as to become real property is called a _____.

Unit 1: Review Exam

1. A parcel of land ½ mile by ½ mile contains how many acres?
    (a) 40
    (b) 120
    (c) 160
    (d) 320

2. An owner-initiated court action seeking fair compensation from the government when an owner's property value has been diminished due to the government's actions is called:
    (a) Inverse condemnation
    (b) A reverse escheat action
    (c) Equitable estoppel
    (d) Special assessment on a redevelopment area

3. Police Power is a governmental right that could result in:
    (a) Exercising the power of eminent domain
    (b) Establishment of zoning standards
    (c) Levying special assessments to build roads
    (d) Taking ownership of property when someone dies without heirs

4. A developer sold off 2 sections of land at the following prices: five 100-acre parcels at $300 per acre and the remainder at $150 per acre. How much revenue did the developer receive from the sale?
    (a) $117,000
    (b) $267,000
    (c) $150,000
    (d) $276,000

5. How many square miles are in a section?
    (a) 1
    (b) 3
    (c) 6
    (d) 36

6. Which of the following has the largest area?
    (a) 4,067 sq yards
    (b) One acre
    (c) 41,167 sq. ft.
    (d) 220' x 190'

7. A road comprising a total of 4 acres runs along the southern boundary of a section. Of the following, which is most nearly the width of this road?
    (a) 20 feet
    (b) 25 feet
    (c) 30 feet
    (d) 33 feet

8. Metes and bounds is used:
   (a) Only on government land
   (b) For description of boundaries
   (c) On unsurveyed land
   (d) With township and ranges only

9. All of the following statements about a property description by metes and bounds are true **EXCEPT**:
   (a) It is used for properties for which no map has been duly recorded
   (b) It is beneficial for its brevity, simplicity, and ease of interpretation
   (c) It is used even though other types of legal descriptions are possible
   (d) It is used to describe irregularly shaped properties

10. What are imaginary lines called that are used in a government survey system for legally describing property, and which are six miles apart?
    (a) Base and meridian lines
    (b) Range lines and township lines
    (c) Longitude and latitude lines
    (d) Metes and bounds lines

11. The N ½ of the SW ¼ of Section 18, R3W, T4N, SBB&M is an example of a legal description by:
    (a) Metes and bounds
    (b) Reference to recorded map
    (c) U.S. Government survey
    (d) Record of survey

12. A parcel of land 100 yards by 100 yards consists of approximately how many acres?
    (a) ¼ acre
    (b) 2 acres
    (c) 20 acres
    (d) 1 acre

13. The build-up of land as the result of action of water is:
    (a) Avulsion
    (b) Accretion
    (c) Dereliction
    (d) Erosion

14. Eminent domain does not apply to:
    (a) Just compensation for the fair market value of the property
    (b) Zoning authority changing the use and therefore the value of the property
    (c) Right of the government to take property
    (d) Condemnation proceedings

15.   If there is a difference between local building codes and the national Uniform Building Code, which would prevail?
        (a)   Local building codes always take precedence over the national Uniform Building Code
        (b)   The national Uniform Building Code always takes precedence
        (c)   The national Uniform Building Code applies only to general code, local codes are more specific
        (d)   Whichever has the higher standards of health and safety will prevail

16.   Which of the following is considered real property?
        (a)   Trade fixtures that can be removed without any damage to the property
        (b)   Mineral rights
        (c)   A refrigerator in a mobile home that is not permanently affixed
        (d)   A crop of tomatoes planted by a tenant

17.   Local zoning ordinances determine the use of land and may also restrict:
        (a)   Size
        (b)   Setbacks
        (c)   Location of buildings
        (d)   All of the above

18.   A distinguishing characteristic of real property as distinct from personal property is:
        (a)   That it is a long-term asset
        (b)   High cost of acquisition
        (c)   Can be depreciated over a useful life
        (d)   Immovable

19.   The power of eminent domain can be exercised by:
        (a)   Cities
        (b)   Public utilities
        (c)   Public education institutions
        (d)   All of the above

Unit 1: Review Exam Key

1. c   A parcel of land ½ mile by ½ mile equals ¼ of a section. A section contains 640 acres.

2. a   Inverse condemnation is a legal action brought by the owner of land when government puts nearby land to a use that diminishes the value of the owners property.

3. b   The government's police power is the basis for zoning ordinances. The taking of private property is based on the government's right of eminent domain. The power of the government to take ownership of private property when someone dies without heirs is called escheat.

4. b   What is the remainder of the land?
         2 sections X 640 = 1280 total acres;
         1280 acres – 500 acres = 780 acres
         Cost of the five 100-acre parcels: 5 X 100 = 500 X $300 = $150,000
         The remainder: 780 acres X $150 = $117,000
         $150,000 + $117,000 = **$267,000**

5. a   A section is 1 mile by 1 mile, or 1 mile square. A township would be 36 square miles.

6. b   One acre equals 43,560 sq. ft.

         4,067 sq yards equals 36,603 sq. ft. (9 sq ft = 1 sq yard)

         220' x 190' equals 41,800 sq. ft.

7.   d   This is a math area problem. The formula for solving this area problem is
Width x Length = Area. The best way to solve area problems is to first draw a diagram:

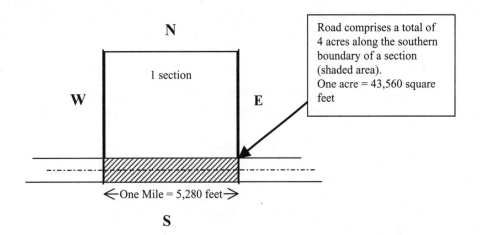

The area is known to be 4 acres or 4 times 43,560 square feet. If the road runs along a section then the road is 1 mile or 5,280 feet long. W x L = Area. We know the length and the area. We are looking for the width.

W   x   L   =   Area

?   x   5,280   =   (4 x 43,560) = 174,240

Divide 5,280' into174,240, which equals 33 feet.

8.   b   Metes and bounds can be used for any type of property, but is normally used when the parcel is irregular and there is no recorded map. The property has to be surveyed in order to know the dimensions and the directions.

9.   b   Metes and bounds descriptions are very beneficial, but are a complex method of land description that is not known for its brevity, simplicity, or ease of interpretation.

10.   b   The township and range lines are the imaginary lines used in a government survey system for legally describing property, which are six miles apart. Be careful, base and meridian lines occur only once in each Base and Meridian where the two lines intersect.

11.   c   The N ½ of the SW ¼ of Section 18, R3W, T4N, SBB&M is an example of a legal description using the U.S. Government Survey system.

12.   b   To find the approximate acres:

Length x Width (100 yards by 100 yards) = square foot area (90,000 square feet)

Divide sq. foot area (90,000) by square feet in an acre (43,560) = 2.06 acres

13.   **b**   Accretion is the build-up of land as the result of the action of water.
Avulsion is the sudden tearing away of land by the violent action of a watercourse.
Erosion is the gradual wearing away of land by current, wind or tide.

14.   **b**   Zoning authority changing the property's use is an exercise of police power (regulation for the common good), and not eminent domain.

15.   **d**   Whichever has the higher standards of health and safety will prevail.

16.   **b**   The right to extract mineral, oil, and gas substances are part of what constitutes real property. Choices (a), (c), and (d) are all examples of personal property.

17.   **d**   The governing authority of a city or county has the power to adopt ordinances establishing zones within which structures must conform to size, setback, and location limitations.

18.   **d**   Real property consists of that which is immovable by law.

19.   **d**   Among those able to exercise the power of Eminent Domain and take private property for a public use are: Government bodies (Federal, State, and local), improvement districts, public utilities, public education institutions, and similar public and semi-public bodies.

Unit 2: Rights and Interests in Land

Lecture Outline and Notes

Key topics in this unit:

- The estate concept of property ownership
- Forms of ownership
- Encumbrances

Reading assignments (in <u>California Real Estate Principles, 6th Edition</u> textbook)

- Chapter 3: Ownership of Real Property
- Chapter 4: Encumbrances

I.   **ESTATES IN LAND**

Estate = As applied to real estate, the degree, quantity, nature and extent of interest that a person has

A.   **Freehold Estates**

Ownership for an unpredictable duration

1.   Fee simple absolute

a.

b.

c.

2.   Fee simple defeasible / Fee simple subject to a condition subsequent

a.   Lasts "so long as" condition is met

b.   Transferable and inheritable

c.   Can revert to grantor if condition is

d.   Requires court action

3. Life estate

   a. "Life tenant" (grantee) is present owner and has use for

   b. Upon death of the designated person, the estate:
      - Returns to grantor
      - Or goes to 3rd party

   c. Life tenant may sell, lease, or encumber the property, but upon the life tenant's death (or the death of whomever is the measuring life), buyer/lessee/lender loses his or her interest.

   d. If life estate is based on life tenant's life, the life tenant's interest can not be willed.

B. **Less-than-Freehold (Leasehold)**

The right of a lessee to possess the lands of a lessor. The lessee holds a leasehold estate.

Statute of Frauds: All transfers of an interest in real estate **must be** in writing **except** a lease of 12 months or less.

A leasehold estate is also known as a "chattel real" –

1. Estate (tenancy) for years

   a.

   b.

   c. Death of lessor/lessee DOES NOT terminate.

2. Periodic Tenancy/ Estate from period to period

   a.

   b. Example: month-to month agreement

   c.

3. Estate at will
   Indefinite duration; terminated by notice or death

4. Estate at sufferance
   a.

   b. If owner accepts payments from tenant at sufferance, estate at sufferance becomes periodic estate.

II. FORMS OF OWNERSHIP / WAYS OF HOLDING TITLE

A. Sole Ownership/Estate in Severalty

1. Property owned solely and separately by one person

2. Upon death, property goes to heirs or devisees.

3. Any single entity, such as a corporation, can hold title in severalty.

B. Multiple Ownership

Two or more persons share ownership, with undivided interests. Because their interests are undivided, they have equal rights of possession; no co-owner has a right to any specific part of the property.

1. Tenancy in common: co-ownership <u>without</u> right of survivorship to other owners

    a. Two or more persons who own undivided interests; may be any fraction of whole

    b.

    c. Co-owners have unity of possession.

    d. Partition lawsuit – court proceeding by which co-owners seek to sever their co-ownership

2. Joint tenancy: co-ownership by natural persons with right of survivorship

    a. All joint tenants share:

    (memory aid **T-T-I-P**)

    b. Must be specified in deed

    c.

    • Upon death of co-owner, interest of deceased is dissolved and goes to co-owners without probate.

    d. If individual co-owner encumbers share and dies, creditor has no claim.

    e. Death certificate and affidavit of death of joint tenant must be filed to obtain marketable and insurable title.

3.   Community Property: co-ownership only available to married couples

      a.   Husband and wife are equal partners in the community property.

- Community property is that which is acquired during marriage.

- Separate property is that which is acquired before marriage or property acquired during marriage by gift, inheritance, or if there is a separate agreement.

- Income from separate property remains separate property unless the finances are commingled.

      b.   For married couples, community property is presumed unless otherwise stated in deed –

      c.   Upon death, surviving spouse retains his/her half interest, with other half going to heirs/devisees of deceased.

      d.   If specifically stated in deed, title can be taken as community property with right of survivorship. This enables surviving spouse to obtain marketable and insurable title without delay and without probate.

      e.   Individual spouse can enter into employment contracts (listing), but both spouses' signatures are required on a sales contract and deed.

Note: Buyers should obtain an attorney's advice to determine the most appropriate form of co-ownership.

4.   Business Ownership

      a.   Corporation

- A "legal person" with perpetual existence

- Can hold title in severalty or as tenant in common, cannot be joint tenant

- Disadvantage is double taxation – corporation and individual shareholders pay tax on money earned.

b.   Partnership

      i.   General partnership

- All partners participate in the operation of the business and may be held personally liable for business losses and obligations

- Single taxation – individual partners file tax returns.

      ii.   Limited partnership

- Assigned general partners and many limited partners

- Limited partners have limited liability according to individual share.

- Limited partners cannot participate in management.

- Single taxation

- Papers must be filed with Secretary of State.

c.   LLC – Limited Liability Company

Most common method used by real estate syndicates

Taxes paid either as partnership or corporation

C. **Common Interest Ownership**

    1.   Condominium

        a.   Real estate, portions of which are designated for separate ownership ("units") and the remainder of which is designated for common ownership and use ("common elements")

        b.   May be applied to any type of real estate

        c.   Each unit owner is a member of the unit owners' association, which has the following functions:

- Manages common elements

- Adopts rules, regulations, budgets

- Charges and collects assessments to pay for association expenses

        d.   Separate title and taxation

- Deed transfers separate, fee simple interest in unit, plus undivided interest in common elements. All unit owners share ownership of common elements.

- Unit together with common element % = separate parcel.

- Taxed as separate parcel.

        e.   Conversion of apartments to condominiums

-

-

2.	Stock Cooperative

    a.	Owned by a corporation, which in turn leases space to stockholders.

    b.	Cooperative corporation (tenants' association) owns the real estate.

    c.	Buyer receives membership in association, shares of stock, and proprietary lease.

    d.	Stockholder/tenant pays assessments and association fees.

3.	Community Apartment Project

    a.	Owner has an undivided interest in the entire property, as a tenant in common with the other owners, and a right to occupy a certain unit.

    b.	Operation, maintenance, and control are usually exercised by a governing board elected by the owners.

4.	Planned Development

    a.	Individual ownership of house and lot, plus common ownership of common areas and membership in association

    b.	Differs from a condominium in that property owners actually own the land beneath their house and the structure, rather than air space of condo unit.

5.	Time shares

    a.	Purchaser receives right to exclusive use of a unit for a particular period of time each year.

    b.	May be an estate interest or a use interest

    c.	Three-day right of rescission on an offer to purchase a time share

III. ENCUMBRANCES

Encumbrance = any claim, right, or interest held by one who is not the legal owner of the property. Encumbrances are imperfections that may negatively affect property value. They may create a cloud on title that may impair or diminish owner's rights.

A. Easement

A non-possessory right to use the land of another for a specific purpose.

1. **Appurtenant easement** has a dominant tenement and a servient tenement.

2. **Easement in gross** has no dominant tenement, only servient tenement. Example:

3. Created multiple ways

   a. Express grant or reservation –

   b. Easement by Prescription/Prescriptive Easement:
   An easement recognized by the courts after fulfilling specified requirements (example: open and notorious occupation for five continuous years)

   c. Easement by Necessity:
   An easement created by court to

4. Terminated multiple ways, depending on how it was created. Examples:

   a. Merger of dominant and servient tenement

   b. Release, for example – by dominant tenement holder with quitclaim deed

   c. Non-use/Abandonment

   d. Quiet title action in court

B.   **Deed Restrictions/Restrictive Covenants/Subdivision Deed Restrictions/ Condominium By-Laws/CCR's (Covenants, Conditions, and Restrictions)**

Privately created limitations on land use, which protect property values and the interests of property owners.

1.

2.

3.   For violating covenants, owners may be subject to injunction or suit for monetary damages.

Not as severe a penalty as for *violating a condition*

4.   Covenants terminated by agreement of benefiting owners and issuance of a quitclaim deed

C.   **Lien**

Makes the property security for the payment of a debt. A lien can be:

- voluntary or involuntary
- general or specific

1.   Government lien for property taxes or special assessments (statutory specific involuntary lien)

2.   Mechanic's lien (involuntary specific lien)

A lien created by statute which exists against real property in favor of persons who have performed work or furnished materials for the improvement of the real property.

a.   Lien rights attach, and priority of the lien is determined, based on when work first began and/or materials furnished.

b.   If there is no written contract, a supplier or subcontractor has 20 days from the time that work begins or material is delivered, to provide preliminary notice of the right to file a lien.

c.   A notice of non-responsibility may be filed by the owner within ten days after receiving notice that protects owner from unauthorized work.

d.   Claimants perfect liens on unpaid work or materials by

- If owner filed notice of completion, lien must be filed within 60 days after that for contractors and 30 days for other claimants.

- If owner did not file notice of completion, lien must be filed within 90 days after completion of work.

e.   A lien release or lien waiver is recorded to terminate a mechanic's lien.

3.   Mortgage/deed of trust lien (voluntary specific lien)

4.   Judgment lien (involuntary general lien)

         a.

         b.   Abstract of judgment is recorded and becomes a lien in all counties in which it is recorded.

         c.   Court issues writ of execution to enforce the judgment.

5.   IRS lien (involuntary general lien) – income or estate taxes

6.   Lis Pendens – A recorded document that gives constructive notice of a pending lawsuit.

7.   Atttachment – a seizure of personal property to satisfy a potential later judgment

NOTE: California Homestead Law allows for a monetary exemption, which protects a person's principal residence, within limits, from a forced sale against certain unsecured liens. <u>A homestead is not a lien or encumbrance.</u>

IV.   ENCROACHMENTS

Unauthorized use of another person's land; physical object intruding onto neighboring property. Disclosed by a survey.

V.   LICENSES

A personal, revocable and unassignable permission to do one or more acts on the property of another without possessing any interest in the property is called a license –

Unit 2: Glossary Review

Verification and recording
Quitclaim deed
Chattel real
Non-use for 5 years
Involuntary, specific lien
License
Freehold estate
Date work began or materials were furnished
Lien
Less-than-freehold estate

1. To release an easement, a dominant tenement property owner can execute a _____.

2. An easement by prescription expires due to _____.

3. Ownership of a condominium is an example of the following kind of estate: _____.

4. Renting an apartment is an example of the following kind of estate:_____.

5. An individual holding a leasehold estate has a _____.

6. _____ are required for mechanics' liens to be valid.

7. A mechanic's lien is an example of an _____.

8. The priority of a mechanic's lien is determined by _____.

9. A personal, revocable and unassignable permission to do one or more acts on the property of another without possessing any interest in the property is called a _____.

10. A claim on land to secure payment of a debt is called a _____.

Unit 2: Review Exam

1. All of the following constitute a lien **EXCEPT** a(n):
    (a)   Mortgage
    (b)   Judgment
    (c)   Attachment
    (d)   Homestead

2. A fee simple estate has all of the following characteristics **EXCEPT**:
    (a)   It is free of all encumbrances
    (b)   It is of indefinite length or duration
    (c)   It can be inherited
    (d)   It is freely transferable

3. A flooring contractor named Harry is hired to install a hardwood floor as part of a new home construction project. If Harry ends up having to file a mechanic's lien on the property his right of priority is established:
    (a)   When construction began on the house
    (b)   When the lien is recorded
    (c)   When the installation of the floor was started
    (d)   When the floor is finished

4. An estate that will last for a period of 6 months only, and that is fixed in advance by a contract between the parties is called a(n):
    (a)   Estate for month to month
    (b)   Periodic tenancy
    (c)   Estate in sufferance
    (d)   Estate for years

5. A court procedure that is used to enforce private restrictions on real property is called a(n):
    (a)   Writ of Execution
    (b)   Injunction
    (c)   Attachment
    (d)   Quiet title action

6. When a person takes title in severalty he or she is taking title:
    (a)   With others as tenants in common
    (b)   With others as joint tenants
    (c)   With others as tenancy in partnership
    (d)   As a sole owner

7. A charge imposed on real property as security for a specific act is the definition of:
    (a)   A deed restriction
    (b)   An attachment
    (c)   A lien
    (d)   Taxes

8.   A court order which applies to all property owned by a person in a specific county is called a:
     (a)   Special lien
     (b)   General lien
     (c)   Voluntary lien
     (d)   None of the above

9.   Which of the following would hold a less-than-freehold estate?
     (a)   Grantees
     (b)   Trustees
     (c)   Lessees
     (d)   Mortgagees

10.   Jones leased a property to Smith for a seven year period. Jones died during the term of the lease. Smith found out that Jones only had a life estate on the property. The new owner wants to cancel the lease. Which of the following is true.
     (a)   The lease terminated on the death of the life tenant.
     (b)   A lease never terminates prior to the end of the term.
     (c)   The new owner is required to act in good faith and renegotiate the lease with the tenant.
     (d)   A lease always takes priority over a life estate.

11.   Regarding an appurtenant easement, all of the following must be true **EXCEPT**:
     (a)   This kind of easement is said to "run with" the land
     (b)   A dominant tenement must be adjacent to and abut the servient parcel on at least one side
     (c)   There must always be a minimum of two parcels under separate ownership
     (d)   The easement right does not terminate due to death, sale, or non-use

12.   All of the following are ways that easements can be terminated **EXCEPT**:
     (a)   Upon destruction of the property which is a servient tenement
     (b)   When an owner of the servient tenement revokes the easement
     (c)   If an owner of a dominant tenement executes and delivers a quit claim deed
     (d)   If a prescriptive easement is not used for five years

13.   Barbara owns an estate in real property that consists of an undivided interest in a parcel of real property as a tenant in common, combined with a separate interest in the air space in a residential unit. Her ownership is described as a:
     (a)   Cooperative
     (b)   Community apartment project
     (c)   Condominium
     (d)   Planned unit development

14.   John and his sister Mary own property as joint tenants. All of John's financial affairs, other than the property, are separate. John died without any other assets, leaving many unsecured debts. John's creditors could:
        (a)   File a lis pendens against the property
        (b)   Bring an unlawful detainer against the sister
        (c)   Get no satisfaction from the real property because upon John's death, the property is owned separately by his sister
        (d)   Get an attachment on the real property

15.   In order to have a joint tenancy, which one of the following <u>has</u> to exist?
        (a)   All parties must live on the property
        (b)   All parties must have equal interests
        (c)   All parties must be single
        (d)   All parties have to commit to ownership for a specific period of time

16.   Which of the following groups of words would not include any general liens?
        (a)   Estate tax lien, corporate tax lien, judgment lien, attachment
        (b)   Attachment, mechanic's lien, mortgage, property taxes
        (c)   Mortgage, trust deed, blanket trust deed, income tax lien
        (d)   Unrecorded mechanic's lien, franchise tax lien, assessments, land contract

17.   Unless there is an express agreement to the contrary in the deed restrictions and plans, which of the following would be considered part of a condominium unit?
        (a)   Swimming pool
        (b)   Heating system for the entire building
        (c)   Elevator
        (d)   None of the above

Unit 2: Review Exam Key

1.   (d)   A lien is a charge upon property for the payment of a debt. Of the choices listed only the Homestead is not a money claim or lien. A homestead is a statutory exemption of real property used as a home from the claims of lien holders up to a specified amount.

2.   (a)   It is possible to own property in fee simple and still have encumbrances on it.

3.   (a)   The effective date of any mechanic's lien relates back to the date construction began on the project.

4.   (d)   Any lease for a definite period of time creates an estate for years, regardless of the period of time for which it was established.

5.   (b)   An injunction is a court order restraining or requiring performance by a party to a suit (such as performing acts required by property covenants or refraining from acts restricted by such covenants).

6.   (d)   The term "severalty" in real estate means one or sole owner.

7.   (c)   A lien can be defined as a charge imposed upon specific property by which it is made security for the performance of an act, typically the payment of a debt.

8.   (b)   A general lien is directed against the individual debtor and attached to all of that person's real property in the county in which the abstract of judgment is recorded.

9.   (c)   Lessees are holders of leasehold estates, all of which are less-than-freehold (estates with limited time durations).

10.   (a)   This question illustrates the rare situation where a lease may be terminated by death. The lessor can lease the property only for the term of his life. Upon the lessor's death, he no longer has an interest in the property and the lessee's interest terminates.

11.   (b)   The dominant tenement may have the right to cross over three or four lots in one tract and not all of the servient tenements would be immediately adjacent (contiguous) or abut the dominant tenement

12.   (b)   The owner of a servient tenement cannot revoke an easement. The owner of a dominant tenement, the parcel receiving the benefit, may terminate by giving a written quit claim deed to the servient owner. Destruction of the servient tenement, by its very nature, would terminate the easement on such a parcel. An easement gained through prescription can be lost through nonuse for five years.

13.   (c)   The Civil Code defines this form of ownership as a condominium. The property could be residential, industrial, or commercial.

14.   (c)   Upon the death of one joint tenant, the interest passes to the survivor free and clear of claims by the creditors. Since the brother's creditors did not institute court action to sell the real property and satisfy their lien prior to his death, they have no right to the title now held in severalty by the sister.

15.   (b)   In a joint tenancy there must be a unity of time, title, interest and possession.

16.   (b)   Choice (b) lists all specific liens. In the other choices, judgment lien, income or estate tax lien, and franchise tax lien are all examples of general liens.

17.   (d)   The swimming pool, heating system for the entire building, and elevator are all parts of the common area.

Unit 3: Title Transfer and Taxes

Lecture Outline and Notes

Key topics in this unit:

- Conveying ownership
- Types of deeds
- The conveyance of ownership after death
- Other ways of acquiring rights in real property
- Escrow
- The requirements for recording documents
- Title insurance
- Taxation

Reading assignments (in <u>California Real Estate Principles, 6th Edition</u> textbook)

- Chapter 5: Transferring Real Estate
- Chapter 6: Escrow and Title Insurance
- Chapter 7: Property Taxation

I.   CONVEYING OWNERSHIP

The act of conveying real estate ownership (title) is called **alienation** (the opposite of acquisition). A **private grant** is from individuals using a deed. A **public grant** is from the government to individuals using a patent. A **dedication** is from individuals to the government.

A.   Documents Used to Transfer Interests in Property

1.   Deed –

2.   Bill of Sale –

B.   **Essential Elements of a Valid Deed**

      1.   In writing

      2.   Competent grantor (Giver is grant<u>or</u>; receiver is grant<u>ee</u>.)

              •

      3.   Must designate a grantee

      4.   Granting Clause (Words of conveyance)

              •

      5.   Adequate description of the property

              •

      6.   Execution (signed) by grantor(s)

C.   **For valid deed to be effective and transfer title it must be:**

      1.

      2.

      NOTE: Not essential for a valid or effective deed: consideration, date, grantee signature, legal description, Habendum Clause ("to have and to hold") or recording.

D.   **Types of Deeds**

      Any deed conveys all interest presently held by the grantor, unless it specifically states that it is conveying a lesser interest.

      1.   Grant Deed (most commonly used deed in California)

            a.   Implied Warranties

                   •

                   •

            b.   Conveys after-acquired title

2.   Quitclaim Deed

       a.

       b.

3.   Gift Deed

4.   Warranty Deed

5.   Reconveyance Deed

6.   Sheriff's Deed

7.   Tax Deed

8.   Trustee's Deed

II.   CONVEYANCE AFTER DEATH

A.   Probate

1.   The judicial process that administers the business affairs of a person who has died. It is subject to the laws of the state in which property is located or where a person is a resident.

2.   Listings – exclusive listings on real property are limited to 90 days.

3.   Commissions – If real property is sold through probate course, real estate licensee's commission is set by *the court*.

B.   Transfer by will (Testate)

1.   Types of wills

       a.   Statutory Will - approved form provided for by statute

       b.   Witnessed Will – more formal, usually created by an attorney

       c.   Holographic will – in testator's handwriting

2.   Transfer of real property by will is called "a devise" (parties – devisor/devisee).

3.   Transfer of personal property by will is called "a bequest," the property itself is referred to as a legacy (parties – legator/legatee).

C. **Intestate Succession**

    1.   When a person dies **without a will** they are said to have died

    2.   Distribution of the estate is governed by the **Law of Succession** when there is no will.

    3.   A person who receives property under the Law of Succession is an **heir**.

III. OTHER WAYS OF ACQUIRING RIGHTS IN REAL PROPERTY

A. Adverse Possession

Ownership recognized by the courts after fulfilling <u>five</u> essential elements:

1.

2.

3.

4.   Held under a claim of right or color of title

- Claim of right – Adverse possessor asserts claim that he/she is the owner.

- Color of title - Holds document appearing to give good title (for example, a forged deed).

5.

B. Easement by Prescription

Right to use another's property recognized by the courts after fulfilling <u>four</u> essential elements:

1.   Open and notorious occupation

2.   Continuous for five consecutive years

3.   Hostile to the true owner's interests

4.   Under claim of right or color of title

C. Public Transfer

1.   From the State –

2.   To the State –

IV.   PUBLIC RECORDING SYSTEM

A.   Recording Process

Policies and procedures that regulate recording are established by **state statute**. In California, each county has a county recorder who is responsible for organizing and maintaining recorded documents.

1.   Note date and time of filing.

2.   Assign recording number.

3.   Copy document into public record.

4.   List document alphabetically in grantor and grantee indexes.

5.   Return original to indicated party.

B.   System allows us to POST claims

1.

2.   Establishes priority of interest –

C.   System allows us to SEARCH claims

1.

2.

D.   Requirements to Deliver Instruments for Recording

Deeds, loan documents, easements, and long-term leases are among the types of instruments that are usually recorded.

Recording does NOT prove the validity of the document.

Instruments to be recorded must be:

1.   Executed (signed)

2.   Acknowledged (notarized)

V.   **HOW MARKETABLE TITLE IS DETERMINED**

Marketable (or merchantable) title is ownership free from reasonable doubt. The buyer's goal is to obtain marketable title.

A.   **Chain of Title**

B.   **Evolution of insuring marketable title through title insurance**

1.   Abstract of Title

2.   Certificate of Title

3.   Guarantee of Title

4.   Title Insurance

C.   **Title Insurance**

Protects an owner or lender up to a specified amount against specified types of loss involving defective or unmarketable title.

1.   Preliminary Title Report and Commitment

a.   States current condition of title

b.   Lists policy exceptions and exclusions: defects and encumbrances that have been discovered or that may exist and which are not covered by the policy

2.   Standard Coverage Policy

California Land Title Association (CLTA) – Limited coverage primarily for owners that insures against losses from:

o   Forgery and fraud

o   Matters of record

o   Improper delivery

o   Lack of capacity

3.   Extended Coverage Policy

American Land Title Association (ALTA) – Additional protection, normally required by lenders, that insures against losses from:

- o   Unrecorded tax and assessment liens

- o   Unrecorded mechanic's liens, easements, or encumbrances

- o   Water rights and mining claims

- o   Correct survey showing encroachments

- o   Rights of parties in possession

4.   A physical inspection will be necessary.

5.   No policy will insure against all risks. Government regulations such as

D.   Quiet Title Action

- •   A court action brought to remove a cloud on the title.

VI.   ESCROW/CLOSING STATEMENTS

A.   Escrow

with instructions, with a neutral third party, to carry out the provisions of a contract

1.   Elements of Escrow

   a.   Seller's deed and buyer's money are deposited with the escrow agent who acts as a stakeholder.

   b.   Escrow agent -

      i.   Agent for both parties while transaction is in progress

      ii.   After close of escrow becomes an agent for each party

      iii.   Must be a corporation <u>except for</u>:

   - Banks, savings and loans, title insurance companies, trust companies, and attorneys

   - Real estate brokers acting in a transaction for which a broker's license is required

2.   Escrow Documents

   a.   Transfer Agreement – Deposit Receipt/sales contract

   b.   Escrow Instructions – A document separate from the contract that instructs the escrow holder to act.

   c.   If escrow instructions and sales contract are in conflict, escrow instructions, being the most recent document, will likely prevail.

3.   Stages of Escrow

   a.   Complete escrow – documents and money have been submitted, waiting to close

   b.   Perfect escrow –escrow has closed

   c.   Termination of Escrow

   d.   Escrow Legally Required

   - Sale of business under Bulk Sales Law

   - Sale of liquor license

   - Court ordered sales, e.g. – probate sales

4.   Resolution of disputes – Escrow agents can only release funds upon:

- Agreement between parties

- Court order – interpleader action

- Arbitration decision

B.   Closing Statements

A detailed accounting of each party's debits and credits (amounts paid and received)

1.   Proration

a.   A calculation on a closing statement that results in buyers and sellers paying only their respective shares of property expenses.

b.   Prorations are based on a **30-day month** and a **360-day year** unless escrow is instructed otherwise.

c.   The day that escrow closes is normally charged to the buyer.

d.   Likely to be prorated:

- Taxes, most of the time

- Rent, if it is income property

e.   Unlikely to be prorated:

- Insurance – Buyer will purchase new policy. If the term of seller's insurance is not complete, insurer may charge **"short rate."** (Example: if full year's policy was $1,000, but policy is cancelled after 6 months, short rate might be $650 dollars for the half-year.)

2.   Proration Method

a.   Establish date for Close of Escrow (**COE**) and Date Item is paid to (**DI**) and compute the time differential.

b.   Determine the monthly cost of the item.

c.   Multiply the monthly cost by the differential…

❑   If **DI** is before **COE**, the seller owes the buyer.

❑   If **DI** is after **COE**, the buyer owes the seller.

Sample Proration Problems:

1. A buyer is purchasing a four-unit apartment building. Monthly rents total $2,350 and are due on the first day of the month. The date of closing is October 18. What part of the October rents is the buyer entitled to receive?

2. Close of escrow on a house is June 16. The sellers have already paid both installments of the fiscal year's tax bill of $1,987.20. What amount will be charged to the buyers?

C. **RESPA (Real Estate Settlement Procedures Act)**

1. Federal law that standardizes closing practices for certain transactions

2. Restricts amount of advance escrow account payments for taxes and insurance

3. At time of loan application (or within three business days afterwards), lender must give settlement costs booklet and
(including loan origination fees).

4. Borrower has the right to inspect Uniform Settlement Statement (HUD-1) one day before closing.

   a. Statement must be delivered by
   to the borrower, at or before closing.

   b. If borrower waives right of delivery, the Uniform Settlement Statement must be mailed

   c. Lenders may not charge a fee for preparing the statement.

5.
   e.g., lenders, insurance agencies, escrow companies, or home protection companies paying money for referrals by brokers.

VII.   TAXATION

A.   Real Property Taxes

1.   An **ad valorem** tax –

2.   Parties involved in property tax process:

Board of Supervisors –

-

County Assessor –

-

County Tax Collector –

-

3.   **Proposition 13**

Limited tax rate to:

- 1% of assessed value, plus
- voter-approved indebtedness

4.   Assessed value of property is its full cash value unless there has been a reassessment event.

Assessment increases are limited to:

- Maximum of 2% per year, or
- When ownership changes, or
- When improvements are made to the property

5.   Appeals of Assessment

- Appeal may be made to

6.   Special Exemptions

        Homeowners – $7,000

        Veterans – $4,000

        Senior Citizens – May postpone paying taxes until they sell

7.   Special Assessments

        Street Improvement Act of 1911:

- Used more than any other law for street improvements ("off-site improvements")
- Appears on property tax bill

        Mello-Roos:

- No requirement that improvements will benefit individual properties
- Unpaid assessments do not appear on property tax bill but are separately levied and collected.
- Seller must disclose if lien exists.

8.   Supplemental Assessments

        All ownership changes must be reported to the tax assessor at the time of recording. The new owner will be taxed, based on a reassessed value, from the date of transfer and will get a supplemental tax bill.

9.   Tax Calendar

    a.   Based on fiscal year, runs from July 1 through the following June 30.

- Taxes become a lien on the January 1st preceding the tax year

    b.   Property Taxes are payable in two installments **(Memory aid: <u>N</u>o <u>D</u>arn <u>F</u>ooling <u>A</u>round)**

- First installment due – **_N_**
- First installment delinquent – **_D_**
- Second installment due – **_F_**
- Second installment delinquent – **_A_**

10. Delinquency

    a. If installment is not paid on or before delinquent date, a 10% penalty is charged.

    b. If taxes are not paid by June 30, the property is declared in default, costs are added and interest is charged from the beginning of the tax year, July 1.

    c. The tax defaulted property is subject to a right of redemption.

    d. Public Auction

- If taxes are not paid for five years, the tax collector publishes a Notice of Intent to Sell.

- The tax collector sells the property for the state at public auction and issues a Tax Deed to the successful bidder.

- Title given is free of all private liens.

B.   County Documentary Transfer Tax

    1.   A county tax paid on most real estate transfers at time of recording.
The tax rate is $.55 per $500.00 or fraction thereof.
It is paid on the total purchase price less any existing loans that are
assumed.

Sample Documentary Transfer Tax Problem – A house is sold for $687,575. An existing first
trust deed of $524,000 is assumed by the purchaser. What amount of documentary transfer tax
may be charged?

C.   California Sales and Use Tax

    1.   Example of a straight tax. The same rate is applied to all taxable
amounts.

    2.   State Board of Equalization

        a.   Collects sales and use tax

        b.   Issues Certificates of Clearance to demonstrate that all previous
sales taxes have been paid

           •   Protects buyer of business from

D.   **Federal Income Tax**

1.   Example of a progressive tax – as taxable income increases, tax rate increases

2.   Classifications of income

-
-

3.   Property classifications

-
-
-
-
-

4.   IRS treatment of profit or loss upon sale of property

Property Classification	Profit	Loss
Personal Residence	Capital Gain	No tax effect
Investment	Capital Gain	Capital Loss
Income	Capital Gain	Capital Loss
Trade or Business	Capital Gain	Ordinary Loss
Dealer	Ordinary Income	Ordinary Loss

5.   Calculation of Gain or Loss

Basis is the net amount a taxpayer has invested in his or her property.

1.   To calculate **Adjusted Basis:**

$$\text{Cost of Acquisition} + \text{Capital Improvements} - \text{Allowable Depreciation}$$

2.   Calculate **Gain** or **Loss:**

$$\text{Adjusted Selling Price (after costs of sale)} - \text{Adjusted Basis}$$

6. Calculation of Book Value of an Asset for Accounting

Original	+	Capital	−	Accumulated
Cost		Improvements		Depreciation

7. Tax Deferment Methods

Generally, gains are subject to income tax in the year in which they occur. In some situations, the IRS will allow the recognition of capital gains to be deferred into the future.

Recognized gain: gain that is taxable in the year of sale

Deferred gain: gain that does not have to be recognized in a given tax year. Tax is deferred to a subsequent year.

Realized gain: total of recognized and deferred gain

Installment Sales: a method of reporting recognized gain and paying taxes, when installments are received, if the sales price is being paid in one or more annual installments after the sale.

Tax Deferred Exchanges (Section 1031 IRS Code)

- Often called "tax-free," but more accurately termed "tax-deferred"

- Must be an exchange of eligible (like kind) property

- The first step in a 1031 Exchange is to balance the equities.

- Taxes are deferred so long as the taxpayer does not receive either of the following:

8.   Depreciation or Recapture of Capital

The IRS allows an investment to be recaptured (returned) out of income during the time an income or business property is owned. This is commonly called "taking depreciation." This is one of a variety of ways that real estate can be used to reduce Federal income taxes - referred to as a "tax shelter."

To take depreciation, the property must have a limited useful economic life (only available on improvements, not available on land) and must produce income.

- Improvements on residential income producing properties have an economic life of 27.5 years.

- Non-residential structures have a 39-year economic life.

- Alternative Cost Recovery System (ACRS) provides a straight-line basis for 40-year period for non-residential property.

E.   Homeowner Tax Advantages

1.   Exclusion on Sale of Principal Residence

     a.   Up to $250,000 for a single person

     b.   Up to $500,000 for a married couple filing a joint return

-

- A taxpayer can only have one principal residence at a time.

- A personal residence is a different tax classification. A taxpayer can deduct mortgage interest payments on two personal residences.

2.   Real Property Tax Deductions

3.   Interest Deductions

    a.   Home Mortgage Interest

        • Up to $1,000,000 for home acquisition indebtedness

        • Up to $100,000 for home equity indebtedness

    b.   Consumer Interest – No longer deductible

4.   Other Tax Issues

    a.   Discount Points

    b.   Loan Origination Fees

    c.   Prepaid Mortgage Interest

    d.   Prepayment Penalty

    e.   Tax Credits:

        Low-income housing credit

        Rehabilitation credit

5.   Report to IRS of Transfers

    a.   Foreign Investment in Real Property Tax Act (FIRPTA)

    b.   Exempt if sales price
        and the buyer intends to

Unit 3: Glossary Review

patent	alienation
deed	exception
grantor and grantee	grantor
delivered and accepted	Street Improvement Act of 1911
recorded	extended coverage (ALTA) policy
grant deed	Short Rate
zoning	standard coverage (CLTA) policy
complete escrow	"boot"
quitclaim deed	Uniform Settlement Statement

1. A written legal document by which ownership of real property is transferred from one person to another is a(n) _____.

2. An original conveyance of title to real property from the government to a private owner is called a(n) _____.

3. The two parties to a deed are the _____.

4. To be valid, a deed must be executed by the _____.

5. Title does not pass to the grantee until the deed is _____.

6. Even though it is not required for validity, in order to give constructive notice that title has passed a grantee would want to have the deed _____.

7. The most commonly used type of deed in California is the _____.

8. A deed that conveys whatever interest in the property the grantor holds at the time of conveyance and contains no covenants or warranties is called a(n) _____.

9. _____ is the opposite of acquisition.

10. A law that authorizes local governing bodies to order street improvements and bill the owners for the work through a special assessment is _____.

11. The type of title insurance that would cover unrecorded liens and encroachments is called a(n) _____.

12. A policy of title insurance that insures against forgery, fraud, and matters of record is a(n) _____ .

13. An item NOT covered by standard or extended title insurance is called an _____.

14. A _____ is one where everything is ready for closing but the transaction has not yet closed.

15.   Insurance companies refer to an insurance policy rate that is used for less than the full term as a _____.

16.   Cash received in a tax deferred exchange is referred to as _____.

17.   Lenders cannot charge a fee for filling out the _____.

Unit 3: Review Exam

1. The county Documentary Transfer Tax is $.55 per $500, or fraction thereof, of equity transferred. If a property sells for $150,000 with $125,000 of cash and new loans and an assumed loan of $25,000, the tax will most nearly total:
    (a) $28.50
    (b) $138.00
    (c) $82.50
    (d) $182.50

2. A real estate agent has a buyer and seller sign escrow instructions and delivers the instructions to the escrow agent. The escrow agent discovers certain discrepancies between the instructions and the purchase contract. Which of the following statements is true?
    (a) The purchase contract takes priority because it is the agreement between the parties.
    (b) The escrow instructions, being the most recent document, will generally prevail.
    (c) The transaction is in jeopardy because the parties are not in agreement.
    (d) The real estate broker must resolve the conflict.

3. Which of the following would normally be short rated in escrow?
    (a) Insurance
    (b) Commissions
    (c) Taxes
    (d) Documentary Transfer Tax

4. The Street Improvement act of 1911 provides that funds may be raised by the local government for all of the following purposes **EXCEPT**:
    (a) Purchase of land for a subdivision
    (b) Paying for streets
    (c) Payment for street lighting
    (d) Pay for sewers

5. If a dispute arises between a buyer and seller during escrow, the escrow holder may legally:
    (a) Make a decision who should get the money.
    (b) Cancel the transaction and return all monies to both parties
    (c) Initiate a court action called specific performance
    (d) Go to court in an interpleader action

6. The county maintains an assessment roll that includes the assessed value of all taxable property:
    (a) To determine the actual tax rate
    (b) To facilitate assessment appeals boards actions
    (c) To equalize assessments
    (d) To establish the total assessed value to determine the "tax base"

7. All of the following instruments are used to transfer interests in real property **EXCEPT**
    (a)   Grant deed
    (b)   Trust deed
    (c)   Bill of sale
    (d)   Contract of Sale

8. Who is entitled to examine the records at the county recorder's office?
    (a)   Title company employees
    (b)   Any interested citizen
    (c)   Real estate licensees
    (d)   Any party to a transaction that has been recorded

9. A standard coverage policy of title insurance insures against the following:
    (a)   Any defects in title known to a purchaser but not known to the title company as of the date of the policy
    (b)   Lack of capacity of persons having to do with title
    (c)   Unrecorded mechanic's liens
    (d)   Rights of parties in possession

10. Who would be in the weakest position against loss of property due to a claim by an outsider?
    (a)   Holder of a recorded deed who is insured under a policy of title insurance
    (b)   Holder of an unrecorded deed who occupies the property
    (c)   Holder of a recorded grant deed who rents the property to a tenant
    (d)   Holder of an unrecorded quitclaim deed who does not occupy the property

11. The capital gain exclusion from taxation on a principal residence is:
    (a) $250,000 for a single person who has lived in the property for one year
    (b) $250,000 for an individual or $500,000 for a married couple but only if one of them is over 55
    (c) $250,000 if the seller purchases another residence of equal or greater value
    (d) $250,000 for an individual or $500,000 for a married couple every two years

12. All of the following are subject to property taxes **EXCEPT**:
    (a)   Vacant lots located in unincorporated areas
    (b)   Intangible personal property, e.g. – ownership of copyrights, trademarks, etc.
    (c)   Possessory interests of lessees in tax exempt publicly owned properties
    (d)   A mobile home that is on a permanent foundation on leased space in a park

13. The annual residential tax obligation is determined by:
    (a)   County Assessor's Office
    (b)   County Recorder's Office
    (c)   County Board of Equalization
    (d)   County Treasurer's Office

14.   "Tax Shelter" is a term most appropriately associated with:
    (a)   Real estate licensee expenses
    (b)   Income Taxes
    (c)   Profit on the sale of vacant land
    (d)   An owner-occupied home that requires a lot of maintenance

15.   Which of the following would be considered recognized gain in a 1031 exchange?
    (a)   Like kind property
    (b)   Decrease in depreciation
    (c)   Mortgage relief
    (d)   All of the above

16.   Roberts sells a house using an installment sale. The major advantage is the ability to:
    (a)   Choose which years he wants to declare his gain
    (b)   Postpone declaring the gain until the debt is fully repaid
    (c)   Pro-rate the gain over the term of the installment contract
    (d)   Declare the gain in the year of the sale

17.   The term "ad valorem" most nearly means:
    (a)   According to value
    (b)   Adjusted basis
    (c)   Adverse possession
    (d)   Assessed value

Unit 3: Review Exam Key

1.   (b) $125,000   ÷   500   =   250
                   250   x   .55   =   137.50
            Closest: $138.00

2.   (b)   A subsequent document (such as escrow instructions) will prevail over an earlier document (the deposit receipt).

3.   (a)   Taxes are usually prorated in escrow. If the seller's insurance is taken over by the buyer, the seller would be credited proportionately (pro rata) for the portion of the premium the buyer is debited for. When the buyer gets new insurance, a seller's policy will be cancelled and a higher premium (called a "short rate") will be charged to the seller for the portion of the term that the seller has used the insurance. The short rate is indicated on a uniform schedule approved by the Insurance Commissioner. The amount paid by the seller, in excess of the short rate, will be returned to the seller by the insurance company.

4.   (a)   The Street Improvement Act of 1911 authorizes the local government to order improvements and pass the expense on to the landowner. This authority cannot be used for the original purchase of the land for a subdivision.

5.   (d)   The escrow holder is really only a stakeholder, not legally concerned with controversies between the parties, and is entitled to bring an interpleader action where the court decides who among the claimants is legally entitled to the property.

6.   (d)   Between March 1 and July 1, the County Tax Assessor compiles a list showing the assessed value of all taxable property in the county (the tax rolls) as of March 1. This total is the "tax base." Using this, and the budget to run the county, the Board of Supervisors sets the tax rate needed to meet the budget, within the limits set by Proposition 13. The County tax Collector applies the rate to each property's assessed value to determine that year's individual property tax.

7.   (c)   A bill of sale is a written instrument by which one person sells, assigns or transfers an interest in personal property to another.

8.   (b)   The records of the Office of the County Recorder are public records, with access available to all persons.

9.   (b)   Among the risks listed in the question, a standard coverage policy of title insurance (CLTA policy) would only protect against persons lacking the capacity to convey title.

10.   (d)   An unrecorded deed is considered void as against a subsequent good-faith purchaser who is without notice and who does record or take possession. The two methods of giving constructive notice of a claim or interest are (1) recording and (2) occupying the property. In choice D, the holder has done neither. In choice A, a policy of title insurance is indicative that the named holder is the owner of record.

11.   (d)   An individual is currently entitled to a maximum exclusion from capital gains of $250,000 ($500,000 for a married couple filing a joint return) so long as the property has been occupied as a principle residence for two out of the last five years.

12.   (b)   Among the choices given in this question, only intangible personal property is exempt from property taxes.

13.   (a)   The annual tax obligation is based on the assessed value, which is determined by the County Assessor's Office.

14.   (b)   Tax Shelter is a term associated with income taxes.

15.   (c)   Mortgage relief is where the loan on the property the person is acquiring is less than the loan on the property that is being disposed of. It is unrelated to depreciation. "Boot" is property that is not of a like kind received in a tax-deferred exchange. It includes cash or it's equivalent, such as a note and trust deed or other personal property. Boot is also taxable as recognized gain.

16.   (c)   Roberts can pay the tax on the proportional amount of gain that he receives in the tax year he receives it.

17.   (a)   Ad valorem means "according to value." This is a method of taxing using the value of the thing taxed to determine the amount of tax.

Unit 4: Real Estate Contracts and Subdivision Laws

Lecture Outline and Notes

Key topics in this unit:

- The essential elements of a valid contract
- How a contract is created
- Types of real estate contracts
- Property Transfer Disclosures
- Subdivision Laws

Reading assignments (in <u>California Real Estate Principles, 6th Edition</u> textbook)

- Chapter 8: Contracts
- Chapter 9: Creating a Leasehold Contract
- Chapter 10: California Subdivision Laws

I. **ESSENTIAL ELEMENTS OF A VALID CONTRACT**

A valid contract is an agreement to do (or not do) a specific thing that the courts will enforce. Four elements are essential for a valid contract:
(Memory aid: CoCa CoLa)

A. **<u>Co</u>nsent/Mutual Agreement**

1. Offer, acceptance, and communication of acceptance, before an offer is revoked. (Death of offeror prior to communication of acceptance terminates offer.)

2. Counteroffer.

3. Contractual intention

4. No fraud or misrepresentation (versus "puffing," which is the act of making a claim that anyone would reasonably understand is not literally true.)

    a. Negligent misrepresentation – No intent to deceive. No criminal penalty but contract can be voidable

    b. Fraud (actual fraud) – Intent to deceive

5.   No duress or menace.
       (No force or threat)

6.   No undue influence.
       (No unfair advantage)

B.   Capacity

1.

2.   Sane

3.   Certain felons deprived of their civil rights lack capacity.

C.   Consideration

1.   Something of value must be exchanged –

2.   Terms associated with consideration:

Good consideration is "love and affection."

Valuable consideration refers to items or services of value.

Sufficient consideration is enough to make a binding contract.

Adequate consideration may be used to determine the remedy available upon default.

D.   Lawful Objective
Legal purpose

II.   STATUS OF CONTRACTS

A.   Valid

B.   Void

Lacks one or more of the essentials of a valid contract.

C.   Voidable

Disadvantaged party is not bound (because of fraud, duress, etc.), but the other is.

D.   Unenforceable

A contract that fulfills all essential elements, but due to the following laws

Statute of Limitations
Sets forth the amount of time the non-breaching party has in which to take legal action against the breaching party:

- Breach of oral contracts – 2 years

- Fraud – 3 years from date of discovery

- Encroachments / Trespass – 3 years

- Breach of written contracts – 4 years

- Lawsuits to recover title – 5 years

- Court judgments – 10 years

Statute of Frauds

Requires certain contracts to be in writing and signed to be enforceable

- Applies to any transfer of interest in real property

- Exception: Leases for 12 months or less

- Also includes debt agreements using real property as security, listing agreements, and agreements that will not be completed within a year

III. HOW A CONTRACT IS CREATED

A. Implied Contract

No implied contracts for transfers of any interest in real estate

B. Expressed (Oral or written) Contract

Bilateral

Unilateral

IV. PERFORMANCE AND DISCHARGE

A. Executory vs. Executed

Executory –

Executed –

B. Addendum

Additional material attached to and made part of a contract

C. Amendment

Changes to existing contract terms by mutual agreement

D. Assignment

E.   Novation

F.   Legal Impossibility

A duty required by the contract cannot be legally performed.

G.   Death

Contract is terminated if no one is left to perform.

H.   Mutual Rescission

The return of all parties to their original position before the contract was executed

V.   REMEDIES FOR BREACH OF CONTRACT/DEFAULT

A.   Acceptance of Partial Performance

Choose not to sue

B.   Unilateral Rescission

One-sided cancellation by the disadvantaged party in a voidable contract

C.   Specific Performance

D.   Actual Damages

Sue for money lost

E.   Liquidated Damages (available only if specified in the agreement)

VI. TYPES OF REAL ESTATE CONTRACTS

A. Purchase Agreement/Deposit Receipt

Also known as: offer to purchase; contract of sale; purchase and sale agreement

1. Purpose: I promise to buy AND you promise to sell.

2. Bilateral: binding on both parties.

3. Parties:
   Buyer – during escrow, buyer holds
   Seller – during escrow, seller holds

4. Essential elements include the buyer's and seller's signatures, property description, price and terms.

5. May include one or more contingency clauses stating that the buyer will not be responsible to complete the purchase under certain conditions.

6. A "time is of the essence" clause requires exact adherence to dates specified.

7. Uniform Vendor and Purchaser Risk Act allows buyer to rescind contract if improvements are destroyed before title or possession has passed, so long as there is no agreement to the contrary. If title or possession has transferred, buyer must continue with transaction.

8. If buyer wants to move into property prior to close of escrow, broker should obtain seller's written consent.

B. Option

Potential buyer purchases the right to buy at a fixed price for a designated period of time.

1. Purpose: I promise to sell IF you decide to buy.

2. Unilateral: binding on seller.

3. Parties

4. Requires consideration

C. **Right of First Refusal**

The right of a person to have the first opportunity to purchase or lease real property

D. **Lease**

Called a "chattel real"

1. Purpose: I promise to let you occupy AND you promise to pay rent.

2. Bilateral

3. Parties

4. Required elements:

    - Parties: Names of lessor and lessee (landlord and tenant).

    - Property: Description of property.

    - Period of time – if over a year, must be in writing

    - Payment – amount of rent

    - Signature of lessor

5. Lessor has reversionary interest, allowing lessor to retake possession upon termination of the lease.

6. Sale of property does not terminate lease.

7.   Types of leases:

Gross/Fixed:

Net:
(property taxes, insurance, maintenance, etc.)

Triple-Net: tenant pays rent plus all expenses.

Percentage: tenant pays base rent + a percentage of gross income/sales

Graduated (step-up/index): includes an escalator clause – rent increases at intervals, and is adjusted based on economic indicators (consumer price index)

Land (ground): rent unimproved property

Sandwich: original lease between Landlord and Tenant 1 after Tenant 1 has sublet to Tenant 2

Sale-leaseback: a financing technique where an owner sells property to an investor and then leases the property back. Converts equity to working capital without giving up possession.

8.   Sublease / Assignment/ Novation

- Tenant may sublease or assign the contract without landlord approval unless lease contract states otherwise.

- A sublease transfers part of the lessee's interest; original lessee remains liable.

- An assignment transfers the entire interest. Assignee is primarily liable. Assignor retains secondary liability unless there is a novation.

9.   Termination of leases

    a.   Expiration/Notice

        Estate for years:

        Periodic Estate:
        Notice equal to lease period but no less than 60 days under certain situations

        Estate at will:
        Death of either party or written 60-day notice

    b.   Surrender

    c.   Abandonment by tenant

    d.   Constructive eviction: lease terminated if lessee must vacate due to lessor's actions or failure to act.

    e.   Eviction

        i.   Landlord must give written Notice to Pay or Quit.

        ii.   If tenant fails to comply, landlord files Unlawful Detainer action seeking an order of eviction.

10.   California Landlord-Tenant Law

     a.   Security deposits

         i.   For residential property, maximum amount of security deposit is equal to three months rent if furnished, two months if unfurnished.

         ii.   Landlord has three weeks to return security deposit, on residential property, and provide written itemized statement for deductions.

         iii.   For commercial property, landlord has 60 days to return deposit after deductions.

     b.   Landlord makes an implied covenant of quiet enjoyment (tenant's right to possession won't be disturbed) and warranty of habitability.

     c.   Landlord has the right of entry for certain purposes; must provide notice except in cases of emergency or abandonment.

     d.   Unruh Civil Rights Act, Fair Employment and Housing Act (FEHA) and Federal Fair Housing Act prohibit discrimination in leasing property except for ability to pay.

E.   Real Property Sales Contract/Contract for Deed

Also known as "land contract" or "installment sales contract"

1.   Purpose: the purchase price is paid in installments and the seller delivers a deed when the final payment is made.

2.   Parties

3.   Legal effect

4.   Seller must use buyer's payment to make any existing loan payment prior to using it for another purpose.

VII.   PROPERTY TRANSFER DISCLOSURES

    A.   **Transfer Disclosure Statement (TDS)**

        1.   A disclosure <u>from sellers</u> <u>and their agents</u> that is required to be given <u>to buyers</u> as soon as practicable before transfer.

            a.   Applies to all 1- to 4-family dwellings

            b.

            c.   Repairs are not required, only the disclosure.

            d.

        2.   Exemptions

            a.   Court ordered sales including foreclosure, bankruptcy and probate

            b.   From one co-owner to other co-owner

            c.   Between family members or in a divorce

        3.   Right to rescind

            a.

            b.

            c.   If TDS is amended, the buyer has the right to rescind.

            d.   If TDS is not delivered, buyer can cancel contract anytime prior to closing.

    B.   **Lead-Based Paint Hazards**

        Residential dwellings built before 1978 are referred to as

        Owners of homes built before 1978 must disclose to their agents and to prospective buyers or renters any knowledge they possess regarding the presence of lead-based paint hazards.

            a.   Buyer or lessee must be given the Environmental Protection Agency (EPA) pamphlet.

            b.   Offer buyers the opportunity to have home tested.

C. **Alquist-Priolo Earthquake Fault Zoning Act**

    1.   Requires sellers and/or agents to disclose if the property is located within a state delineated earthquake fault zone

- Fault zone =

    2.   Law requires local agencies to regulate structures built within the zones – only single-family, wood-frame or steel-frame houses up to 2 stories, and not part of a development, are exempt.

    3.   ***Properties built before January 1, 1960.*** A seller of such property must give the buyer a booklet titled <u>Homeowner Guide to Earthquake Safety</u>. If built after January 1, 1960, the home is presumed to be up to earthquake standards.

D. **Comprehensive Environmental Response Compensation and Liability Act (CERCLA)**

    1.

    2.   Imposes liability for environmental problems on anyone who "touches the property" (for example:

E. **California's Environmental Hazards Pamphlet**

    1.   Seller or seller's agent may give buyers a pamphlet prepared by the State of California, "Environmental Hazards: A Guide for Homeowners, Buyers, Landlords, and Tenants," which:

        a.   Identifies common environmental hazards

        b.   Describes the risks involved

        c.   Discusses mitigation techniques

        d.   Provides list of publications and sources

        e.   Provides general information on hazardous wastes

    2.   If the pamphlet is delivered to prospective buyers, neither the seller nor seller's agent has a duty to provide further information concerning hazards, other than lead, unless they possess actual knowledge.

F.   Natural Hazards Disclosure Statement

California real estate transactions require additional natural hazard disclosures, including whether the property is located in a:

- Federally designated flood hazard area

- Very high fire hazard zone

- Earthquake fault zone

- Seismic hazard zone

G.   Megan's Law

Requires every lease, rental agreement and purchase contract for residential property to include a written notice about how to access the registered sex offenders database.

H.   Mello-Roos

Seller of a 1- to 4-unit dwelling must disclose if property is subject to a Mello-Roos lien.

I.   Structural Pest Control Reports (Termite reports)

Licensed structural pest control operators routinely inspect and issue a report on wood destroying pests and organisms in residential property when it is sold. Sellers and agents must disclose and deliver copies of all reports of which they are aware.

J.   Frequency of Flooding

Local agencies may issue a flood hazard report using the following terminology:

Frequent flooding may occur, on average,

Infrequent flooding may occur once in ten or more years.

VIII. SUBDIVISION LAWS

A. Subdivision Map Act

1. Part of California Government Code. Gives local governments control over the physical aspects of subdivisions.

2.

3. Subdivider submits maps (parcel map, tentative map, final map) to obtain local approval. Requires Environmental Impact Reports (EIR).

4. Final map includes any dedications.

B. Subdivision Lands Law

1. Part of California Business and Professions Code. Prevents fraud, misrepresentation and deceit on the public in the marketing of subdivisions, of five or more parcels.

2. Certain "turnkey" projects are exempted.

3. Requires a series of reports

    a. Preliminary Public Report allows developer to accept reservations. Any deposits are fully refundable on demand.

    b. Conditional Public Report allows developer to enter into binding contracts.

    c. Final Public Report is required prior to sale and must be signed by buyer to show receipt.

C. Interstate Land Sales Full Disclosure Act (ILSFDA)

1. Federal law requires approval for small number of subdivisions and regulates sale of unimproved residential lots sold in interstate commerce.

2. Subdivision is exempt if all lots are 20 acres or larger.

3. Registration and disclosure requirements apply if subdivision has 100 lots or more. California Final Report satisfies disclosure requirements.

4. Gives buyer a right of rescission if property has not been inspected by buyer or if property report was not received.

Unit 4: Glossary Review

voidable
net lease
meeting of the minds
vendor/vendee
percentage lease
Superfund Law
tenant
gross lease
valid
consideration
real property sales contracts
terminated
Transfer Disclosure Statement

1. A lease where the tenant pays some or all of the expenses in addition to the rent is called a(n) _____.

2. A lease where a tenant pays a fixed amount of rent and the landlord pays all expenses is referred to as a(n) _____.

3. If an offeror dies prior to communication of acceptance the offer is _____.

4. If a contract is made under duress the contract is _____.

5. The contractual requirement of consent can also be referred to as a _____ _____.

6. A voidable contract is _____ until it is rejected by the injured party.

7. The words valuable, good, sufficient or adequate are types of _____.

8. In a land contract the seller is referred to as the _____ and the buyer is referred to as the _____.

9. Land contracts are also referred to as _____.

10. Agents are not supposed to fill out the seller's portion of the _____.

11. A lease based on the gross income of the lessee is called a _____.

12. The Comprehensive Environmental Response Compensation and Liability Act (CERCLA), to clean up uncontrolled hazardous waste sites, is referred to as the _____.

Unit 4: Review Exam

1. Broker Nguyen listed and negotiated the sale of a home for Seller Ortiz, who was a young married man. At the time of the sale there was no reason for Broker Nguyen to be concerned with the client's age. After the deed was executed and delivered and the escrow closed, the title company notified Broker Nguyen that Seller Ortiz was under 18 years of age. The deed is:
    (a) Valid
    (b) Void
    (c) Unlawful
    (d) Unenforceable

2. If a person signs a contract when they are under duress the contract is:
    (a) Void
    (b) Unenforceable
    (c) Voidable
    (d) Unlawful

3. Tenant Robert Wei is delinquent in his rent under a written lease. Landlord Vicki Sanchez may evict him by:
    (a) Recording a notice of eviction
    (b) Posting a thirty day notice on the tenant's door
    (c) Asking the Sheriff to eject the tenant
    (d) Bringing an unlawful detainer action in court

4. The replacement of an existing contract with an entirely new contract is called:
    (a) Assignment
    (b) Revocation
    (c) Novation
    (d) Hypothecation

5. A contract is said to be executed when it is:
    (a) Completed and fully performed by both parties
    (b) Unenforceable
    (c) Notarized and recorded
    (d) The result of a novation.

6. All of the following parties could normally sue for specific performance **EXCEPT**:
    (a) An attorney-in-fact operating under a general power of attorney
    (b) An executor of an estate
    (c) A purchaser of a single family residence
    (d) A real estate broker acting as an agent for a principal

7. Of the following, which would not be an essential element for the formation of a contract?
    (a) Mutual consent
    (b) Consideration
    (c) Lawful object
    (d) Performance

8. There can be many reasons why a contract may be voidable in nature. A voidable contract is, however, binding on the parties until it is:
    (a) Adjudicated by a court of law
    (b) Estopped
    (c) Rescinded
    (d) Bilaterally rejected

9. A buyer makes an offer to a seller on a house. Before the buyer is advised of the seller's acceptance of the offer, the buyer can withdraw his offer:
    (a) Only if the contract provides that offers are revocable
    (b) If the buyer enters into a subrogation agreement with the seller
    (c) Only if the offer is not presented to the seller in a timely manner
    (d) For any reason

10. Contracts signed under duress would be:
    (a) A failure of consideration
    (b) Contrary to law and therefore unenforceable
    (c) Voidable
    (d) Valid unless the injured party was a minor

11. A tenant enters into a lease where the terms of the lease provide that the tenant is responsible for the payment of rent plus some property expenses such as taxes and insurance. This kind of lease is referred to as a:
    (a) Net Lease
    (b) Gross Lease
    (c) Lease with an escalator clause
    (d) Sandwich Lease

12. A seller may keep the buyer's deposit as liquidated damages if:
    (a) That is stated in the listing agreement.
    (b) The seller and broker agree.
    (c) The buyer defaults and the purchase agreement stipulates liquidated damages as a remedy.
    (d) The seller failed to perform an essential element of the contract.

13. Under the Uniform Vendor and Purchaser Risk Act, if property is destroyed after a purchase agreement is signed but before the buyer takes possession or title is transferred:
    (a) The buyer must proceed with the purchase.
    (b) The seller may cancel the agreement and retain the earnest money.
    (c) The buyer may cancel the contract and have the earnest money returned.
    (d) The buyer's insurance company must pay for the loss.

14. Smithson signed a purchase agreement to buy Cornell's home. Cornell then decided not to sell his home. Smithson sued him and ended up with the house. Which remedy did she choose?
    (a) Unilateral rescission
    (b) Mutual agreement
    (c) Specific performance
    (d) Damages

15. To comply with the Statute of Frauds, certain contracts must be:
    (a) Written by an attorney
    (b) Acknowledged
    (c) In writing
    (d) Accompanied by earnest money

16. The landlord has not paid the utility bills for his apartment building, so the heat, water, and electricity are shut off. Because of this, the tenants have the right to terminate their leases. Which of the following legal concepts does this example illustrate?
    (a) Constructive eviction
    (b) Mutual rescission
    (c) Illegal use of rent money
    (d) Eminent domain

17. A buyer's offer to purchase states that it will remain open five days for acceptance. Three days after the offer was presented, and before acceptance, the buyer wants to withdraw the offer. The agent should inform the buyer that:
    (a) The offer must remain open for two more days
    (b) Withdrawal of the offer will result in the loss of earnest money
    (c) The buyer is permitted to withdraw the offer prior to communication of acceptance
    (d) The seller may sue for specific performance

18. A contract that has not yet been fully performed is:
    (a) Unenforceable
    (b) Voidable
    (c) Executory
    (d) Executed

19. Joe Tenant signed an apartment lease with Larry Landlord with a three-year term. Joe then sublet the apartment to Sarah Subtenant. As a result of the sublease, the original lease between Joe and Larry is called a:
    (a) Dual lease
    (b) Joint lease
    (c) Sandwich lease
    (d) Percentage lease

20. A real estate contract with an incompetent would be:
    (a) Voidable
    (b) Unlawful
    (c) Unilateral
    (d) Illegal

21. The concept of quiet enjoyment refers to:
    (a) When a neighbor institutes a nuisance suit against another tenant
    (b) A landlord's implied covenant that a tenant's right of possession will not be disturbed
    (c) A government's noise abatement ordinance
    (d) All of the above

22.   Lessee Sanchez may be justified in abandoning his rental dwelling if "constructive eviction" by landlord Chang occurs. Which of the following would constitute constructive eviction?
   (a)   A tenant causes excessive wear and tear to property and the landlord fails to repair the damage
   (b)   A landlord fails to provide water and heat to units
   (c)   A landlord sells the building
   (d)   A condemnation proceeding is initiated by local government under the power of eminent domain.

23.   In a real estate sale transaction the escrow company received two termite reports with different estimates of the cost of repairs. Under these circumstances:
   (a)   The seller has the right to decide which report to use
   (b)   The seller and broker should present both reports to the buyer
   (c)   The buyer has the right to decide which report to use
   (d)   The most expensive report is required to be used

24.   The remedy of unlawful detainer is one that would be used most commonly by an offended:
   (a)   Mortgagor
   (b)   Payor
   (c)   Lessor
   (d)   Lessee

Unit 4: Review Exam Key

1.   (a)   The deed would be valid. Persons under 18 who are married are emancipated minors and have the legal capacity to deal in real property.

2.   (c)   When the mutual consent to a contract is induced by fraud, duress, menace, or undue influence, the contract is voidable at the option of the wronged party. While such a contract is unenforceable against that wronged party, the contract is not totally unenforceable because it is enforceable against the other party. Therefore, choice © is the best answer.

3.   (d)   When a tenant has breached the lease or rental contract by not paying rent, the landlord must institute an unlawful detainer action in court. Part of this procedure is to give the tenant a three-day written notice but the action has to go through court.

4.   (c)   The word novation comes from the Latin words meaning to make new.

5.   (a)   When applied to contracts, the word "executed" means "fully performed by both parties." It can also mean signed.

6.   (d)   A broker acting as an agent in a real estate transaction would not normally be able to sue for specific performance because the broker is not a party to the contract or authorized to bring legal actions.

7.   (d)   Choices (a), (b), and (c) are all essential in the creation of a contract. Performance is the desired result and not essential in the formation of the contract.

8.   (c)   Voidable means the contract is binding until some action is taken to rescind the contract.

9.   (d)   An offer may be withdrawn (revoked) by the offeror anytime prior to the communication of the acceptance by the offeree regardless of the offeror's reason.

10.   (c)   Contracts that are created under duress are voidable, which is to say that only the injured party has the ability to declare the contract void.

11.   (a)   A Net Lease is a lease in which the lessee pays rent and some expenses. A Triple Net Lease is where the tenant typically pays maintenance, insurance and taxes.

12.   (c)   If a buyer defaults and the buyer and seller have separately initialed the liquidated damages clause then the agreement between the buyer and seller is that the seller shall retain the buyer's deposit money as liquidated damages.

13.   (c)   The Uniform Vendor and Purchaser Risk Act is a law providing that the buyer can either cancel the contract and receive his or her deposit money back or proceed with a transaction and receive the seller's insurance proceeds upon the destruction of the improvements prior to close of escrow, so long as the buyer has not taken possession. If the buyer has taken possession then the buyer would have to look to his insurance to recover any loss.

14.   (c)   A successful specific performance lawsuit results in the defaulting party being required to perform as agreed in the contract.

15.   (c)   The Statute of Frauds requires real estate contracts (except leases for one year or less) to be in writing in order to be enforceable.

16.   (a)   In a constructive eviction, the tenant terminates the lease because the landlord has caused or permitted a substantial interference with the tenant's use and enjoyment of the property.

17.   (c)   In general, any offer may be withdrawn prior to communication of acceptance.

18.   (c)   Prior to execution (meaning being fully performed), the contract is executory.

19.   (c)   The original tenant is "sandwiched" between the landlord and the sub-tenant.

20.   (a)   Minors, incompetents, and felons lack capacity to contract and should they enter into a contract it would normally be voidable at the option of the potentially injured party.

21.   (b)   In every lease the law implies a covenant (promise) on the part of the lessor to the "quiet enjoyment" and possession of the property by the lessee during the term of the lease. It is a warranty by the lessor against the lessor's own acts, not those of strangers (i.e.-neighbors).

22.   (b)   The landlord is not obliged to repair excessive wear and tear caused by the tenant. He is obliged to keep the dwelling in habitable condition.

23.   (b)   If two or more inspections exist, all reports must be disclosed. The results of a pest control inspection report, including the cost of corrective work, would be material facts to a buyer and must be disclosed. Who will pay for the repairs is an issue that should be included in the contract.

24.   (c)   When preceded by a three-day notice, unlawful detainer is the proper procedure designed by law, by which the lessor can have the tenant evicted.

Unit 5: Finance

Lecture Outline and Notes

Key topics in this unit:

- Financing instruments
- Foreclosure
- Sources of real estate loans
- Government financing programs
- Government regulations on financing

Reading assignments (in California Real Estate Principles, 6th Edition textbook)

- Chapter 11: Financing Real Estate
- Chapter 12: Government-Sponsored and Other Financing

I.   **FINANCING INSTRUMENTS**

      A.   **Promissory Note**

            A personal property instrument that:

              1.   establishes a promise to repay a debt, and

              2.   identifies:

- the borrower and lender
- amount of the debt
- terms of repayment
- interest rate

The promissory note is:

-

- Secured by mortgage or trust deed

-

  - An unconditional promise signed by the maker (borrower) to pay a certain sum under set terms to the payee (lender/ bearer)

  - A "holder-in-due-course" receives the note in good faith ("innocent purchaser"); enjoys a favored position because maker cannot refuse to pay based on personal defenses. Payee is the endorser.

Sometimes promissory notes are sold for less than their face amount. This is called

---

Sample Discounted Note Problem:

A seller takes back a note secured by a second deed of trust for $11,000 and sells it immediately for $7,000. What is the amount of discount on the note?

B.   **Mortgage and Deed of Trust**

NOTE: The terms "Mortgage" and "Deed of Trust" (or Trust Deed") are often used synonymously. They are not the same, although they do have many elements in common.

- Security instruments that pledge (hypothecate) property as security for repayment without giving up possession

- Include covenants – causes of foreclosure

    o   Non-payment of principal & interest

    o   Non-payment of taxes

    o   Inadequate or no insurance

    o   Waste

- Common Clauses

    Acceleration clause

    Alienation/Due on Sale clause prevents assumption without lender's consent.

    Subordination clause changes order/priority of liens.

    Power of Sale clause allows lender to foreclose through trustee's sale procedure instead of judicial foreclosure.

C.   **Mortgage**

- Two-party instrument that creates a lien on real property pledged as security for a debt.

- Parties: Borrower = Mortgag<u>or</u>
  Lender = Mortgag<u>ee</u>

- Most common financing instrument in the United States.

- California favors Deeds of Trust.

D.   Deed of Trust / Trust Deed

A three-party instrument used instead of a mortgage to create a lien.

Parties: Borrower =
          Lender =
          Third party =

1.   Borrower (trustor) conveys bare legal ("naked") title to third party (trustee) to hold on behalf of the lender (beneficiary) as security for the loan.

2.   Trustor retains what is called an equitable title, and enjoys possession of property and all other rights, so long as he or she does not default.

3.   Trustee may sell property by power of sale in case of default.

II.   SATISFACTION vs. ASSUMPTION

A.   Satisfaction / Reconveyance

1.   When paid in full, mortgage is "dead."

2.   Mortgagee gives "satisfaction of mortgage" to mortgagor.

3.   When trust deed is paid in full:

a.   Beneficiary notifies trustee to reconvey bare legal title.

b.   Trustee executes and delivers to trustor a

B.   Assumption vs. Subject to (Existing Loan Remains in Place)

1.   If buyer purchases property "subject to" a mortgage:

●

●   Seller, not buyer, would be liable for any deficiency judgment.

2.   If buyer assumes, buyer becomes primarily liable for the debt, but the original borrower retains secondary liability.

3.   There are no loan origination fees or points when borrower assumes or purchases subject to a mortgage. There may be an assumption fee.

III. FORECLOSURE

    A.   **Judicial (court action) Foreclosure Process**

        1.   Mortgagee initiates foreclosure suit.

        2.   Mortgagor's right to reinstate

            a.   Borrower can exit foreclosure process through

            b.   Lasts until the foreclosure decree is issued

        3.   Court issues foreclosure decree

            •   Borrower no longer has right to reinstate, only has right of redemption.

        4.   Foreclosure sale

            a.   Property sold at public auction.

            b.   Highest bidder given certificate of sale.

            c.   Excess sale proceeds belong to mortgagor.

            d.   Insufficient sale proceeds may result in deficiency judgment.

        5.   Statutory redemption period: mortgagor's right to redeem after foreclosure sale.

            a.   Mortgagor may redeem by paying entire loan obligation plus all expenses.

            b.   Time period:

                ▪   3 months if no deficiency judgment is available

                ▪   12 months if deficiency judgment is available to lender

        6.   If borrower does not redeem within statutory time period, Sheriff issues Sheriff's deed transferring title to high cash bidder.

        7.

    B.   **Private Sale Foreclosure Process**

        1.   Beneficiary notifies trustee of default, and instructs trustee to record "Notice of Default."

        2.   Trustee records Notice of Default

            •   Three-month period must pass before advertising notice of sale can commence.

3. After three months, trustee can initiate advertising notice of sale.

    a. Must advertise once a week for three weeks

    b. Record at county recorder a minimum of 20 days prior to the date of sale.

    c. Post on the property.

    d. Post in a public place.

    e. Mail notice of sale to trustor, junior lien holders, and anyone who has recorded a request for notice of sale.

4. Trustor's right of reinstatement

- Lasts until five days prior to the date of the sale

5. Trustor's right of redemption

- Is only the last five days immediately preceding date of sale

- There is no post-sale right of redemption.

6. Day of sale, trustee issues trustee's deed conveying title to high cash bidder.

- No deficiency judgment available to beneficiary

C. Deed in Lieu of Foreclosure (Alternative to Foreclosure)

1. Borrower deeds property to lender to avoid foreclosure with permission of the lender.

2. Does not wipe out junior liens.

D. Bankruptcy

Places an automatic stay (hold) on all credit proceedings until released by the bankruptcy court

IV. METHODS OF PRINCIPAL and INTEREST (DEBT SERVICE) PAYMENT

A. Three Basic Methods

1. Term (straight) loan

    a.

    b.

2. Fully amortized loan

    a.

    b. Balance decreases with each payment.

    c. Balance becomes zero at maturity.

3. Partially amortized (balloon) loan

    a. Equal payments of principal and interest, for a set period (for example, 15 years)

    b. With a lump sum "balloon" payment, due in 15 years

Sample Interest Problems:

1. A straight loan has 10% per annum interest and $50 monthly interest payments. How much is the principal on the loan?

2. Raul took out a $14,000 loan for 90 days. He paid $120 interest. What was the annual interest rate?

B. **Alternative Repayment Plans**

Adjustable-rate mortgage (ARM)

    a. Interest rate is subject to change based on economic index plus a margin.

    b. May include payment caps and/or rate caps.

Graduated payment mortgage (GPM)

    a.

    b. May have negative amortization.

    c. Payments may level off after three to seven years.

Graduated Payment Adjustable Rate Mortgage (GPARM)

    Same as GPM, except payments may continue to change based on index, rather than leveling off.

Reverse annuity mortgage

    a. Mortgagee pays the mortgagor monthly payments.

    b. Repaid upon death of mortgagor, or sale of property, or when the balance reaches the maximum limit

V. **SOURCES OF CAPITAL FOR REAL ESTATE LOANS - PRIMARY MORTGAGE MARKET**

A. **Commercial banks:** business and construction loans (also home loans)

B. **Home mortgage lenders**

    1. Savings and loans

    2. Mortgage companies

        a. Mortgage bankers loan their own money.

        b. Mortgage brokers act as intermediaries between borrowers and lenders.

    3. Large real estate investors

        a. Life insurance companies, credit unions, pension funds

        b. Participation loans and investments in income-producing properties

VI.   TRUST DEED / MORTGAGE TERMS

Loan-to-Value Ratio

- Also called a mortgage ratio.

- Maximum percentage of value lender will loan borrower in a particular transaction.

- Usually 80% to 95% on residential loans

Credit Rating

Discount Points

- Money paid to a lender to obtain a loan at a stated rate

- One point = 1% of loan amount.

-

- Paid by buyer or seller at closing

Loan Origination Fee

Charge by a lender to process and issue a loan.

Equity

Market value today
– Total debt today
Equity

Subordination

A clause in a mortgage or agreement, in which the mortgagee permits a subsequent mortgage to take a higher priority position

Prepayment Penalty

Charge paid to a lender by a borrower for paying off a loan prior to its maturity date (considered punitive interest)

Lock-in Clause

A clause in a promissory note, prohibiting buyer from paying the loan off early

Beneficiary Statement

Statement from a lender

Nominal Interest Rate

VII.   TYPES OF TRUST DEEDS / MORTGAGES

A.   **Package**

1.   Personal property is included as security in addition to real property

2.   May be used to finance the purchase of a furnished condominium, etc.

B.   **Blanket**

1.   More than one property pledged as security

2.

3.   Releases are not necessarily in equal amounts; i.e., first parcel released will usually be a greater amount.

4.   Upon repayment of a portion of the loan, the borrower's equity in the still encumbered property increases.

C.   **Open-end**

1.   A loan arrangement where additional amounts may be lent in the future without affecting the loan's priority.

2.   Additional amounts are limited to the difference between the original loan amount and the current amount owed.

D.   **Conventional / Insured conventional**

1.   Repayment of the debt rests solely upon the borrower's ability to repay. No government guarantee or government insurance

2.   Loan default insurance protects lender from loss due to non-payment.

3.   On insured conventional loans, borrower pays private mortgage insurance premium (PMI) to MGIC (Mortgage Guarantee Insurance Corporation) to protect lender against losses due to non-payment.

E. **Construction**

    1.

    2.   Available in installments (obligatory advances) as improvements are completed

    3.   Typically adjustable rate/short term from commercial banks

    4.   Lender may require a commitment for "take-out." A take-out loan replaces the construction loan with longer-term financing.

F. **Wraparound**

    1.   Junior financing that includes the remaining first mortgage balance, which the buyer does NOT assume.

    2.   Buyer pays second lender (typically the seller) who makes payments on the first mortgage.

G. **Purchase money**

A trust deed or mortgage given as part or all of the purchase price. No deficiency judgment is available on one- to four-unit, owner-occupied property. A refinance is not purchase money and a deficiency judgment is available, even on owner-occupied property

H. **Seller Carry-Back Purchase Money**

    1.   Owner financing where title transfers to buyer

    2.   Seller "takes back" a trust deed/mortgage as partial payment. Seller has lien.

VIII. GOVERNMENT FINANCING PROGRAMS

  A.   **FHA-Insured Loan Program (Federal Housing Administration)**

     1.   Loan funds come from approved lenders.

     2.

     3.   (MIP) pays for

                                  (MMI)

               –

     4.   Higher loan-to-value ratio than conventional mortgage is permitted.

     5.   Property must comply with "MPRs"

  B.   **VA-Guaranteed Loan Program (Veterans Administration)**

     1.   VA guarantees lenders against losses on loans to eligible veterans or their qualified dependents.

     2.   Veteran must occupy the property as a home.

     3.   Loan-to-value ratio can be up to 100%.

     4.   Loan amount cannot exceed "CRV" (Certificate of Reasonable Value).

     5.   VA requires Certificate of Eligibility on veteran purchaser.

  C.   **Cal-Vet (California Veterans Farm and Home Purchase Act)**

     1.   California Department of Veterans Affairs administers the program.

     2.   The DVA purchases the property, and then resells to veteran on a real property sales contract.

           a.   Veteran has equitable title – State of California holds legal title.

           b.   Veteran receives legal title when the loan is paid in full.

           c.   Requires impound accounts and cannot have prepayment penalty.

     3.   Veteran is required to acquire a life insurance policy that pays off the loan in case of death.

IX. SECONDARY MORTGAGE MARKET

A. Secondary Market Activities

1. Buying mortgages from primary market lenders to supplement the mortgage and lending process

2. Mortgage-backed securities are sold to investors –

3. To verify the loan balance when purchasing the loan, secondary market purchaser will ask for a beneficiary statement, giving the remaining principal balance and other pertinent information on the loan.

B. Three Main Organizations

1. Federal National Mortgage Association — FNMA ("Fannie Mae"): privately owned corporation that backs all types of mortgages.

2. Government National Mortgage Association — GNMA ("Ginnie Mae"): an agency within HUD that backs residential loans.

3. Federal Home Loan Mortgage Corporation —FHLMC ("Freddie Mac"): a privately owned corporation that mainly buys conventional mortgages from S&Ls and commercial banks.

X. THE FEDERAL RESERVE BANK (THE "FED")

The nation's central bank, charged with regulating the nation's money supply.

> The U.S. dollar's
> can be found by looking at

A. Regulates rate of growth/inflation by:

1. Regulating the reserve requirements of banks

   a. Increases reserve requirements to "stem" (slow) inflation

   b. Decreases reserve requirements to stimulate economic growth

2. Setting the "discount rate" – interest charged to member banks

   a. The Fed raises rate to stem inflation/slow growth

   b. The Fed lowers rate to stimulate growth

3. Buying or selling government bonds

   a. The Fed buys bonds and banks receive an influx of cash to make more loans.

   b. The Fed sells bonds and takes money from the economy – slows growth.

XI.   **CONSUMER PROTECTION LAW**

A.   **Truth in Lending Act (Regulation Z)**

Purpose: Federal law to promote the informed use of consumer credit by insuring that prospective borrowers receive disclosures of loan terms and costs before entering into a credit transaction.

1.   Applies to all real estate loans EXCEPT:

   a.   Loans to corporations

   b.   Business or commercial loans

   c.   Seller financing (purchase money mortgage or contract for deed)

2.   Disclosure requirements

   a.   Total finance charge includes nominal interest, origination or assumption fee, borrower-paid points, mortgage insurance costs. (Closing expenses, legal fees, and title insurance premiums are NOT included in total finance charge.)

   b.   Annual percentage rate (APR), also known as effective rate, expresses relationship of total finance charge to loan amount.

3.   Advertising requirements

   a.   Price and/or APR are the only specific finance terms allowed in advertisement without triggering full disclosure requirement.

   b.   Downpayment, interest rate, monthly payments, or number of payments trigger full disclosure requirement.

Unit 5: Glossary Review

fully amortized loan
guarantees
term loan
redemption
balloon
blanket trust deed
acceleration clause
equity
purchase money mortgage
graduated payment loan
secondary mortgage market
legal title
insurance

1. The borrower's right to pay the entire loan balance plus costs, in order to keep the property, in a foreclosure is known as the right of _____.

2. The clause that appears in both the note and the mortgage, which allows the lender to demand immediate payment of the entire debt if the borrower defaults, is known as an

   _____.

3. A loan that is repaid in one single lump sum at the end of its life is called a straight loan or a _____.

4. A loan in which payments are scheduled so the entire principal balance is repaid by the maturity date is known as a _____.

5. A final payment that is larger than preceding payments is known as a _____ payment.

6. When more than one property is pledged as security for a single loan, the trust deed is known as a _____.

7. A mortgage given by the purchaser to a lender in partial payment for the property is known as a _____.

8. The difference between a property's market value and the debts against it is known as

   _____.

9. A loan that allows a borrower to make smaller payments initially and to increase their size gradually over time is a _____.

10. _____ is where loans are bought and sold.

11. Under a Cal-Vet loan, the Department of Veterans Affairs holds _____.

12. The Veterans Administration _____ loans.

13. FHA is a program that provides loan _____ for lenders to encourage them to make loans that they otherwise would not make.

Unit 5: Review Exam

1. Which terms are closest in meaning?
   (a) Mortgagor — lender
   (b) Mortgagee — borrower
   (c) Lender — mortgagee
   (d) Borrower — lender

2. Subordination means:
   (a) to pay off a loan sooner than required.
   (b) to waive priority of a claim in favor of another lender.
   (c) to sell a loan in the secondary mortgage market.
   (d) renegotiating for a lower interest rate on a mortgage.

3. The three party instrument in which real property is used as security for a loan is a:
   (a) bill of sale.
   (b) chattel agreement.
   (c) certificate of title.
   (d) trust deed.

4. When a holder sells a note for less than its face value it is called:
   (a) taking a loss
   (b) discounting
   (c) yield
   (d) redemption

5. A trustor who wishes to give up title rather than face foreclosure could:
   (a) record a notice of default.
   (b) offer the beneficiary a deed in lieu of foreclosure.
   (c) file a surplus money action.
   (d) file a deficiency judgment.

6. To increase the money supply, the Federal Reserve might choose to lower the:
   (a) mortgage interest rate
   (b) consumer price index.
   (c) reserve requirements
   (d) qualifying ratios

7. A type of mortgage in which more than one property is used as security and that contains a "partial release" clause is a:
   (a) blanket loan.
   (b) package loan.
   (c) purchase money mortgage.
   (d) swing loan.

8.   Discount points:
      (a)   increase the lender's yield
      (b)   lower the lender's yield
      (c)   have no effect on the lender's yield
      (d)   hypothecate the lender's yield

9.   Under FHA loans, borrowers pay:
      (a)   MMI
      (b)   MPRs
      (c)   CRV
      (d)   DVA

10.   An owner's equity in his or her property is best described as the:
      (a)   difference between the market value and the amount owed.
      (b)   difference between the original purchase price and the amount owed.
      (c)   current market value of the property less the owners basis in the property.
      (d)   tax assessor's estimated value less the total outstanding debt against the property.

11.   Rapp is in default on a mortgage. The loan balance is $80,000. The current value is
      $50,000 and the property sells at the sheriff's sale for that amount. A deficiency
      judgment is available to the lender. How long will Rapp's redemption period be for?
      (a)   Three months following the date of the sale
      (b)   12 months following the date of the sale
      (c)   Up until 5 days prior to the date of the sale
      (d)   60 days

12.   MPRs are normally associated with which kind of loans:
      (a)   Cal Vet
      (b)   VA
      (c)   FHA
      (d)   Conventional

13.   A Beneficiary Statement in a real estate loan transaction refers to:
      (a)   the Uniform Settlement Statement
      (b)   the principal amount that is due on a loan
      (c)   a subordination clause
      (d)   appraisal and credit report fees

14.   If a broker talked about the "nominal rate" of a loan he or she would be referring to the:
      (a)   Annual Percentage Rate
      (b)   Federal Funds Rate
      (c)   interest rate indicated on the note
      (d)   effective interest rate

15.   An advertisement shows *only* the annual percentage rate. What else must also appear?
       (a)   Amount or percentage of the downpayment
       (b)   Terms of repayment
       (c)   The fact that the rate may be increased
       (d)   No further disclosure is necessary

16.   Developer Ortiz is setting up a release schedule under a blanket encumbrance. The beneficiary, New Orient Commercial Bank, wants to require a proportionately larger amount of money to release the first lot that is sold in the development. The following are reasons that New Orient wants the larger payment on the first lot, **EXCEPT**:
       (a)   Because the best lots usually sell first
       (b)   So there will be better security on the remaining lots
       (c)   To make sure the developer is financially secure before granting the loan
       (d)   To protect the investment as individual lots are sold

17.   In a promissory note the exact language that would result in all borrowers being committed to repaying the loan would be:
       (a)   Joint tenancy
       (b)   Solely and severally
       (c)   Jointly and severally
       (d)   Jointly and solely

18.   Miguel Sanchez, a developer, wants to purchase some vacant land and have the owner carry back a loan. He wants to get another loan in the future to pay for improvements he wants to make on the land. A clause that would be the most beneficial to Sanchez, the developer, in the original deed of trust used to purchase the land would be a:
       (a)   Partial release clause
       (b)   Due-on-sale clause
       (c)   Release of lien clause
       (d)   Subordination clause

19.   If Ali Musharraf has a loan with an interest rate of 8% per annum and is paying interest of $60 per month, what is the amount of the principal on the loan
       (a) $7,200
       (b) $6,000
       (c) $9,000
       (d) $90,000

20.   A low loan-to-value ratio indicates:
       (a)   A small amount of equity
       (b)   A high amount of equity
       (c)   A high risk loan
       (d)   A government insured loan

Unit 5: Review Exam Key

1. (c) The lender is the mortgagee; the borrower is the mortgagor.

2. (b) In a subordination clause, the first trust deed holder agrees to assume a lower priority position.

3. (d) The document with which real property is made security or collateral for a debt is the trust deed.

4. (b) Discounting a note is where a holder sells the note for less than its face value.

5. (b) A deed in lieu of foreclosure stops the foreclosure process by transferring ownership of the property from the borrower to the lender. The lender must agree to this course of action.

6. (c) The Federal Reserve can increase the money supply and stimulate the economy by decreasing the reserve requirements, lowering the discount rate or buy bonds.

7. (a) A blanket mortgage covers two or more parcels of real estate. A partial release clause releases part of the property from the trust deed upon partial payment of the debt.

8. (a) Discount points are an amount deducted in advance by a lender from the principal amount of a loan as part of the cost to the borrower of obtaining the loan. Discount points increase the lender's yield.

9. (a) In loan insured by the Federal Housing Administration (FHA) the borrower must pay Mutual Mortgage Insurance (MMI) in order to obtain the loan. The property must qualify for the loan by possessing certain Minimum Property Requirements (MPRs). In a loan guaranteed by the Department of Veterans Affairs (DVA) the required government appraisal of the property is called a Certificate of Reasonable Value (CRV).

10. (a) Today's value minus today's debt equals today's equity.

11. (b) The statutory redemption period for a loan that is foreclosed through judicial (court action) foreclosure and sells at a sheriff's sale is 12 months, if a deficiency judgment is available to the lender (if the property sells for less than the loan obligation).

12. (c) FHA will insure a loan only if the property meets MPRs, which stands for Minimum Property Requirements.

13. (b) A "Beneficiary's Statement" (a.k.a.: "Bene" Statement) is a statement issued by a lender giving the remaining principal balance and other information concerning the loan. Escrow agents usually request this statement when an owner wishes to sell the property, or assume, refinance, or pay off an existing loan.

14. (c) The nominal interest rate is the rate indicated (named) in the note and is also known as the contract rate.

15. (d) If only the APR is given, no additional disclosures are required.

Don't confuse this with the following rule: If **any** of the following are given:
- Amount or percentage of any downpayment
- Number of payments or period or repayment
- Amount of any payment
- Amount of any finance charge

Then, the ad **must** disclose:
1. Amount or percentage of the downpayment
2. Terms of repayment
3. APR, and if the rate may be increased, this must be stated

16. (c) Choices (a), (b), and (d) are all legitimate reasons for the release schedule to be out of proportion on the sale of the first lot. Choice (c), borrower qualification has nothing to do with a release clause.

17. (c) "Jointly" means the creditor can look to all of the signers as a group; "severally" means the creditor can look to any one signer for the entire amount due. Co-signers on a note are "jointly and severally" liable.

18. (d) Since construction lenders require first priority, the previously recorded trust deed must have a clause that requires it to "relinquish priority" to a subsequent trust deed.

19. (c) Formula is: **Rate**   **X**   **Principal**   **=**   **Interest**

12 mos x $60/mo = $720 annual interest

$$.08 \quad X \quad ? \quad = \quad \$720$$

$$\$720 \quad \div \quad .08 \quad = \quad \$9,000$$

20. (b) A low loan-to-value ratio indicates a high equity. A loan-to-value ratio of $60,000 on a $100,000 value is lower than one of $80,000 on $100,000. In the first instance, the owner has an equity of $40,000; in the second instance, the equity is only $20,000.

Unit 6: Appraisal

Lecture Outlines and Notes

Key topics in this unit:

- Value concepts
- The appraisal process
- Three approaches to estimate value
  - Sales Comparison
  - Cost
  - Income

Reading assignments (in <u>California Real Estate Principles, 6th Edition</u> textbook)

- Chapter 13: Real Estate Appraisal

I. **VALUE**

    A. **Definitions**

Appraisal = A written estimate of the market value of a specific property on a stated date, by a qualified (licensed, certified, and impartial) appraiser.

- An appraisal is considered valid only for the exact date specified.

NOTE: A real estate licensee can perform a competitive market analysis, but should not refer to it as an appraisal.

Cost = a historic figure that represents the amount of labor, material, and capital to create a property

Price = a present amount established by what a buyer pays for a property today

Value = what a thing is worth

B.   **Market Value – Objective (value in exchange)**

The highest price (in terms of cash or its equivalent) that a property should bring when:

1.   a willing seller would sell and a willing buyer would buy;

2.   the property is exposed on the open market for a reasonable time;

3.   both parties are familiar with the property's uses, defects, and advantages; and

4.   neither is under abnormal pressure to sell or buy.

C.   **Utility Value – Subjective (value in use)**

•   The value that a property possesses in relation to satisfying the desires of an individual purchaser for a particular use of the property

D.   **Four Essential Elements of Value** (Memory aid is **D-U-S-T**)

_**D**_

_**U**_

_**S**_

_**T**_

E.   **Forces that Influence Value**

•   Environmental and Physical Characteristics –

•   Social Ideals and Standards

•   Economic Influences

•   Political or Governmental Regulations

F. **Principles of Value**

1. Highest and best use

    a.

    b. Produces greatest net return over time to the land.

    c. Not necessarily present use.

    d. Must be financially feasible, legally permitted, and take into account adjacent land uses.

2. Substitution

    a.

    b. The value of property is set by the cost of acquiring an equally desirable substitute property

        • If identical properties are for sale, demand is greatest for the lowest priced.

        • May be in terms of use, design, or income.

    c. The basis for the sales comparison approach; however, it is used in all three appraisal approaches

3. Supply and demand

    a. Supply: number of available properties (of a certain type in a certain area).

    b. Demand: number of properties that will be purchased.

    c. Large quantity for sale, price goes down –

    d. If scarce and desired, price goes up –

4. Contribution

    a. A component part of property is valued in proportion to its contribution to the value of the whole property.

    b. Increasing returns: improvements add more value than they cost.

    c. Decreasing returns: improvements add less value than they cost.

5.   Conformity

    a.   Maximum value is realized when a reasonable degree of economic and social similarity prevails in an area

    b.   Monotonous uniformity reduces value

6.   Regression

A property of higher value tends to decrease when surrounded by properties of lesser value (under-improvement).

7.   Progression

The value of a property of lesser value tends to increase when surrounded by properties of greater value (over-improvement).

8.   Change

Neighborhoods go through a life cycle of growth, stability, decline, and revitalization.

9.   Anticipation

    a.   Basis for the income approach

    b.   Value is created from the anticipation of future benefits

10.   Competition

    •   Profit tends to breed competition and excessive profit leads to ruinous competition

11.   Balance

Maximum value is created and maintained when the four agents in the production of income are in balance

    a.   Land
    b.   Capital
    c.   Labor
    d.   Management

G.   Factors that Affect Individual Property Value

<u>Assemblage</u>

a.   When two or more parcels are combined into one ownership, the resulting parcel can have a value that is greater than the sum of the individual parcels

b.   —

the increase in value that results from an assemblage of parcels

<u>Action of the sun</u>

a.   A major consideration in site selection for a retail store

b.   Shady side of the street (south and west) has the most demand for retail use.

<u>Frontage</u>

a.   The linear distance that a parcel of land faces a street

b.   Differs from width or length which could be larger or smaller than the frontage

<u>Front foot</u>

a.   A term used for sale or valuation purposes of retail or commercial property based on how much frontage the property has.

b.   The property is said to have a value based on a certain amount of "dollars per front foot."

- Not used on residential property that is normally said to have a value based on a certain amount of "dollars per square foot."

II. PURPOSES VS. FUNCTION OF APPRAISALS

Purpose and function of an appraisal are not the same thing.

The purpose of an appraisal is always to estimate value.

The function of an appraisal is the intended use of the appraisal or the reason the appraisal was requested. Uses of appraisal include:

- Transferring ownership of property
- Financing and credit
- Taxation
- Insurance purposes
  Condemnation actions

III. TYPES OF APPRAISAL REPORTS

A. The Uniform Standards of Professional Appraisal Practice (USPAP) govern the conduct of appraisers.

1. Established by The Federal Institutions Reform, Recovery and Enforcement Act

2. Appraisals for federally-related loans (includes most residential loans) must be performed by state-certified and licensed appraisers.

3. California licensing requirements:

   a. "Residential" appraisal licenses may appraise residential property (1-4 units) up to a transaction value of $1 million.

   b. "Certified residential" appraisers may appraise all residential property, and nonresidential property up to a transaction value of $250,000.

   c. "Certified general" appraisers may perform all appraisals.

B. Three types of appraisal reports under USPAP:

Restricted Use Report (Letter Form Report)

Summary Report (Short Form Report)

Self-Contained Report (Narrative Report)

- The most detailed and complete form of report
- Type of value being sought is found in the

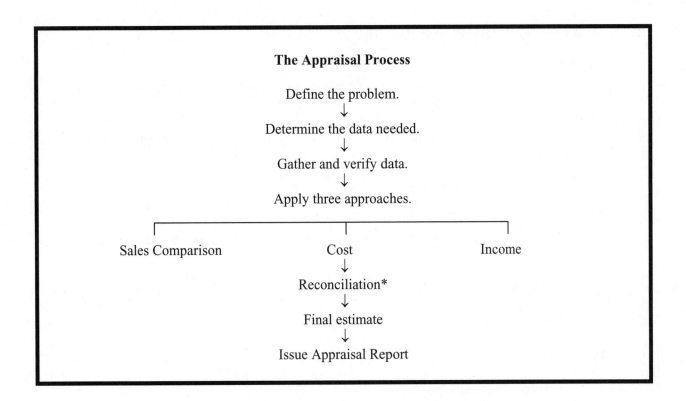

*Reconciliation – the same as correlation (NOT averaging), bringing together the estimates from the three approaches to value; sales comparison, cost, and income approach, and weighing each to generate a final estimate of value

IV.   **SALES COMPARISON APPROACH**

- Also called market data or market approach.

- Most important method for single-family homes, known as amenity-type property, and for vacant land.

Estimate of value (typically a value range) is based on adjusted sales prices of similar properties that were recently sold.

A.   **Evaluate subject property**

B.   **Compare similar properties that have sold recently ("comps" or comparables)**

C.   **Primary Elements of Comparison**

1.   Location in the neighborhood

2.   Date of sale

3.   Amenities

4.   Exterior dimensions of improvements (square footage)

D.   **Adjustments**

1.

2.   Reconcile (never average) the adjusted prices.

V. **COST APPROACH**

Most important method for unique or special-purpose properties (churches, city hall, post office) and is **very accurate** on new construction. **Normally sets the upper limit of value**

Value = Cost to build new − Accrued depreciation + Land value

A. **Cost to Build New**

1. Reproduction cost new

   – same quality of workmanship, materials, design and layout - a duplicate

2. Replacement cost new

3. Determining cost (five methods):

   Quantity survey

   - Most accurate method
   - Determine quantity of all materials, labor and profit

   Unit-Cost-in-Place

   - Second most accurate method
   - Installed price of components (walls, roof, etc.)

   Square foot

   - Less accurate
   - Square footage of space is multiplied by the cost per square foot
   - Normal method used in California, mainly for residential properties, for example:

   Cubic foot

      Similar to square foot method; often used for industrial or warehouse buildings

   Index

   - Easiest method but least accurate
   - Appraiser multiplies the original cost of the subject property by a factor that represents the percentage change in construction costs.

B. **Analysis of Accrued Depreciation**

Depreciation is a loss of value for any reason. Depreciation affects only improvements –

Age-Life (a.k.a. "Straight-Line") method of calculating accrued depreciation:

1. Determine economic life

2. Determine cost to replace improvements new today

3. Divide cost by economic life

4. Multiply by effective age = total accrued depreciation

Observed Condition method:

1. Observe deficiencies.

2. Calculate their costs-to-cure.

C. **Categories of Accrued Depreciation**

Physical deterioration (deferred maintenance)

- Wear and tear, e.g. – worn carpets, roof leaks

- Curable or incurable

Functional obsolescence

- Design/outdated equipment, e.g. – obsolete furnace, poor floor plan

- Curable or incurable

Economic obsolescence (also called locational obsolescence or external obsolescence)

-
  Examples: next to airport, bad neighborhood, or local government taking a portion of a property to widen a roadway, resulting in a loss of value to the remaining property

- Always incurable

VI.   INCOME APPROACH

Most important method for income-producing properties

A.   Capitalization of Net Income

A process of converting a future income stream into an expression of present value

- Four-step procedure for determining Net Operating Income (NOI):

    1.   Estimate annual potential gross income (as if fully occupied).

    2.   Estimate Effective Gross Income (EGI) by making deductions for vacancies and uncollectible rents.

    3.   Subtract allowable expenses.

    4.   Result is net operating income (NOI).

        NOTE: Cash flow = net operating income minus debt service (not used in appraisal analysis)

- The IRV Formula for capitalization of net operating income:

$$
\begin{array}{rl}
& \text{Potential Gross Income} \\
& \underline{-\ \text{Vacancy} + \text{Credit Loss}} \\
& \text{Effective Gross Income} \\
& \underline{-\ \text{Expenses}} \\
\text{NOI} \;=\; & \text{Net Operating Income}
\end{array}
$$

R   =   Capitalization Rate

V   =   Value

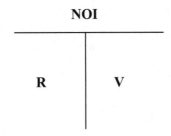

- Establishing a capitalization rate

    a.   Compare the rates of similar properties whose net operating income and value can be determined.

    b.   The quality of income is based upon the financial responsibility of the tenants, which directly influences risk.

    - o

        - o   A start-up business (example: an internet café) would have a higher "cap rate" than a government building (example: a post office)

    c.   If the capitalization rate increases and the income remains the same, then the value of the property decreases.

Sample Problems
Capitalization of Net Income

1. Mr. Singh is interested in purchasing a four-unit building that has a net income of $60,000. Other similar properties, in the area, have sold with a capitalization rate of 10%. What is the indicated value of the property?

2. A property is worth $300,000 with a 6% capitalization rate. What would it be worth if the capitalization rate were 8%?

- Land residual method

    a. Used to find the value of land when there are no good comparable sales of vacant land

    b. Can only be used when the value of the entire property is known, and there is a known value of the building

- Building residual method

    a. Used by an investor to determine how much he or she should spend to construct a building

    b. Can only be used when the value of the entire property is known, and there is a known value of the land

B.   Gross Rent Multiplier

1. Simplified alternative to capitalization that takes into account gross income but not vacancies, bad debts, or expenses. Used primarily for single-family rental homes and smaller income producing properties.

2.   Formulas:

Annual Gross Rent Multiplier × Annual Potential Gross Rent = Value

or

Monthly Gross Rent Multiplier × Monthly Potential Gross Rent = Value

---

Sample Problem
Gross Rent Multiplier

Appraiser Chien knew that her subject property, a single-family residence, was renting for $640 per month. She also determined that a comparable home across the street sold recently for $90,000 and had been renting at the time of the sale for $600 per month. The loan on the property was $68,000. Based on this data, what did Chien determine that the appraised value of the subject property should be?

C.   4 – 3 – 2 – 1 Rule (for commercial property)

1.   40% of value exists in 1st 25% of property depth

2.   As depth decreases – overall value decreases, value per front foot decreases, and square foot value increases.

3.   As depth increases – overall value increases, value per front foot increases, and square foot value decreases.

Unit 6: Glossary Review

Market data approach   Functional obsolescence
Cost approach   Economic obsolescence
Capitalization of net income   Narrative report
Replacement cost   Land
Reproduction cost   Progression
Value   Effective Gross Income
Regression   Reconciliation
Statement of Purpose

1. The most detailed and complete report an appraiser would use is called the
_____.

2. In a narrative appraisal, the type of value being sought would be found in the
_____.

3. The process of converting a future income stream into an expression of present value is called
_____.

4. _____ is the cost of replacing the subject improvement with one that is the exact replica, having the same quality of workmanship, design and layout to duplicate an asset.

5. The cost of replacing a structure with one having utility equivalent to that being appraised, but constructed with modern materials and according to current standards, design and layout is called
_____.

6. _____ involves depreciation based on factors outside the property (e.g., the prosperity of the neighborhood).

7. The cause of depreciation that involves factors having to do with outdated design on the property (e.g., a single car garage, old-fashioned bathroom fixtures, poor floor plan, no air conditioning, over-improved property, etc.) is called _____.

8. A method of valuing a property by comparing the subject property to similar properties that have recently sold is the _____.

9. The _____ is the best method for estimating the value of a house to be built on vacant land.

10. In the cost approach, an appraiser calculates the accrued depreciation of only the improvements. _____ is not depreciated.

11. Demand, utility, scarcity and transferability are essential elements of _____.

12. _____ is potential gross income less vacancy and uncollectible rents.

13. _____ is the same as correlation-bringing together estimates from the sales comparison, cost, and income approaches and weighing each to generate a final estimate of value.

14. An appraisal principle that holds that a higher-valued property in a neighborhood of lower-valued properties will decrease due to association with the lower-valued properties is called _____.

15. The principle that is opposite of regression is called _____.

Unit 6: Review Exam

1. In appraising a 12-year-old, single-family home in a residential neighborhood, which approach would be most applicable?
    (a)   Market data approach
    (b)   Cost approach
    (c)   Income approach
    (d)   Gross rent multiplier method

2. If the cap rate (the capitalization rate) increases, the value of the property:
    (a)   increases
    (b)   decreases
    (c)   stays the same
    (d)   None of the above

3. A property has a value of $130,000 and cap rate of 7%. What would its value be if the cap rate were 10%?
    (a) $143,000
    (b) $117,000
    (c) $91,000
    (d)   Need more information

4. A five-bedroom home with one bath is an example of:
    (a)   functional obsolescence
    (b)   physical deterioration
    (c)   economic obsolescence
    (d)   gross rent adjustment

5. All of the following are examples of obsolescence **EXCEPT**:
    (a)   neighborhood blight
    (b)   an impractical floor plan
    (c)   a two-story home with one bath located in the basement
    (d)   a leaky basement

6. Of the following appraisal terms, which is not an element of value?
    (a)   Demand
    (b)   Scarcity
    (c)   Utility
    (d)   Expectation

7. Functional Obsolescence would not be attributable to which of the following?
    (a)   a home with a ballroom
    (b)   a bathroom off the kitchen
    (c)   Lack of air conditioning
    (d)   Proximity of nuisances in the neighborhood

8. Capitalization is best defined as:
    (a) A relationship between gross income and net worth
    (b) A factor that indicates what a property will produce in monthly gross income
    (c) The result of dividing net income by a percentage rate of return to determine value
    (d) The highest and best return an investor can expect

9. In a narrative appraisal report (referred to by USPAP as a Self-Contained Report), the property value and the type of value would be found in:
    (a) Comments section
    (b) Description of Improvements
    (c) Statement of Purpose
    (d) Reconciliation

10. An appraiser is employed by the owner of an apartment building to determine whether it would be justified financially to add a swimming pool to the apartment complex. The appraiser would want to take into consideration the following appraisal principle in his analysis:
    (a) Principle of Highest and Best Use
    (b) Principle of Contribution
    (c) Principle of Supply and Demand
    (d) Principle of Change

11. The best appraisal method to use to estimate the value of a vacant lot would be:
    (a) Using the age-life method
    (b) Using a gross rent multiplier
    (c) Sales comparison approach
    (d) Quantity survey method

12. Appraiser Ortiz is hired to make a site valuation based on its highest and best use. There is a worthless shack on the land. Appraiser Ortiz should:
    (a) Appraise the value of the land making a deduction for the cost of demolition of the worthless shack
    (b) Appraise the land and the shack with a comment that the shack should be torn down
    (c) Appraise for the value of the land and add the cost of the demolition of the shack to the value of the land
    (d) Tell the owner to tear the shack down before he does the appraisal so it doesn't detract from the value

13. When appraisers appraise property using comparable sales prices of similar homes the adjustments for the differences between the subject property and the comparable are made by adjusting the:
    (a) Subject property to the comparables
    (b) Comparables to the subject property
    (c) Subject property to equal the norm
    (d) Comparable properties to equal the norm

14. Which of the following market conditions might result in decreasing the usefulness of the market comparison approach to appraisal?
    (a) New appraisal licensing requirements
    (b) Rapidly changing political factors
    (c) New types of loan programs being offered
    (d) Rapidly fluctuating economy

15. Whenever it is possible land value should be estimated on the basis of:
    (a) Utility value
    (b) Capitalization of potential income
    (c) Economic life
    (d) Selling price of comparable sites

16. Functional obsolescence is best described as a decrease in value due to:
    (a) External factors beyond the owner's control
    (b) Reaching the end of the physical life of the building
    (c) Property becoming outdated
    (d) Economic deterioration of the neighborhood

17. Appraiser Soon is hired to appraise a residence built in 1910. The owner wants to know how much insurance to take out in case it burns down. Which of the following would Appraiser Soon be likely to use in his appraisal?
    (a) A market comparison of the cost-of-living index of 1910 compared to today
    (b) An original cost of all the materials multiplied by today's cost of living index
    (c) The principle of anticipation
    (d) Today's cost of reproduction

18. The period during which site improvements contribute to the value of the property is called the:
    (a) economic utility
    (b) asset investment life
    (c) accrued depreciation period
    (d) economic life

19. When a large quantity of an item is available for sale, the general opinion is that the price of the item will decrease. However, if the item is relatively scarce and desired, the price will increase. This is an example of which economic principle?
    (a) Supply and demand
    (b) Highest and best use
    (c) Substitution
    (d) Conformity

20. Jose Duarte is considering purchasing a commercial property. The present owner, Shiva Parander, is negotiating with two different prospective tenants, the United States Post Office and a start-up business that wants to operate an oxygen bar. If seller Parander leases to the Post Office, purchaser Duarte would typically use:
    (a) A higher capitalization rate because the government is slow to pay
    (b) The same rate because there is no difference in capitalization rates based on the nature of the tenant
    (c) A lower capitalization rate because there would be less risk
    (d) A capitalization rate based on the rate for the previous owner.

Unit 6: Review Exam Key

1. **(a)** The market data approach is the most important one for the appraisal of single-family residences.

2. **(b)** There is an inverse relationship between the capitalization rate and the property value.

3. **(c)**

R	x	V	=	I
.07	x	$130,000	=	?
.07	x	$130,000	=	$9,100
.10	x	?	=	$9,100
.10	x	91,000	=	$9,100

4. **(a)** Inadequate design or equipment is functional obsolescence.

5. **(d)** A leaky basement is an example of physical deterioration (not functional or economic obsolescence).

6. **(d)** Expectation is not one of the elements of value. The four elements of value (which can be remembered with the memory aid *DUST*) are:
   *D*emand
   *U*tility
   *S*carcity
   *T*ransferability

7. **(d)** Undesirable or unattractive nuisances outside a property would be economic obsolescence

8. **(c)** The process of capitalization of net income is "dividing net income by a percentage rate of return to determine value." The capitalization rate is the relationship between value and net income, not net worth.

9. **(c)** The beginning or cover letter in a narrative form of appraisal sets forth the purpose of the appraisal and the final opinion of value. Everything that follows in this most comprehensive form of appraisal is the appraiser's data to support the appraiser's conclusion.

10. **(b)** The appraiser will endeavor to determine if the additional investment in the improvement will yield a higher net return, that is, will it "contribute" to a greater yield

11. **(c)** The sales comparison approach lends itself well to the appraisal of land, residences and other types of improvements that exhibit a high degree of similarity, and for which a ready market exists

12. **(a)** An appraiser making a site valuation would estimate the value of the lot at its highest and best use. A structure that prevents the highest and best use of the site is an under-improvement, with negative value. The cost of demolition of such a structure would be deducted from the value of the lot at its highest and best use, to establish present value.

13.   **(b)**   In using the comparison approach, an appraiser adjusts the comparable properties to the subject property in order to compensate for the differences.

14.   **(d)**   Rapidly changing economic conditions may limit the usefulness of the sales comparison approach.

15.   **(d)**   Comparable sales data for estimating the value of land should be used "whenever possible"; that is, when there are an adequate number of recent sales in a given area with which to make a comparison.

16.   **(c)**   Functional obsolescence results from outdated design or equipment on the property. It results neither from physical wear and tear nor from external influences

17.   **(d)**   The appraiser is interested in today's cost (less depreciation) to arrive at value. He or she is not concerned about the original cost or any cost of living index.

18.   **(d)**   The economic life of a property is the period of time over which improvements to real estate contribute to property value.

19.   **(a)**   Generally value tends to go up and down with demand and move opposite of supply.

20.   **(c)**   The quality of income is based upon the financial responsibility of the tenants which directly influences risk. The higher the risk, the greater the capitalization rate. The lower the risk, the lower the capitalization rate.

Unit 7: The Law of Agency and Fair Housing

Lecture Outline and Notes

Key topics in this unit:

- Agency relationships
- Agency agreements
- Commissions
- Brokerage
- Trust funds and record keeping
- Mortgage loan brokerage
- Franchise investment law
- Fair housing laws

Reading assignments (in <u>California Real Estate Principles, 6<u>th</u> Edition</u> textbook)

- Chapter 14: The Law of Agency
- Chapter 15: Fair Housing Laws

I. **AGENCY RELATIONSHIPS**

One party employs another to act on his or her behalf.

A. **Parties to an Agency Relationship**

Client/Principal: one who employs another to act on his or her behalf.
Principal is referred to as a "client."

Agent/Fiduciary

- An agent is one who is employed to represent a principal.
- Only a real estate broker can be an agent for a principal/client.

Third party: one with whom agent conducts business on behalf of the principal

Subagent: one who is appointed to act as an agent for the agent

- An associate licensee of a broker is not an agent or subagent of the public.
- When a cooperating broker is appointed as a subagent by the listing broker with the express or implied authority of the seller, the cooperating broker becomes the subagent of the seller.

B. **Broker/Associate Licensee/Client Relationship**

1. The broker represents the client and owes full fiduciary duties to client.

2. Associate licensees (can be either salesperson or broker licensees) are employees of the broker, and owe duties to the client equivalent to the duties owed by the broker.

C. **Fiduciary Duties owed to Principal (Memory aid – OLD CAR)**

O

    a.   Must obey lawful instructions of client

    b.   If prior to listing, a potential client asks broker to do something illegal, broker should decline the listing.

L

D

C

A

R

D. **Agent's Duties to Third Parties (Customers)**

1. Honesty and fair dealing

2. Disclosure of material facts

3. Reasonable care and skill

E.   Scope of an Agent's Authority

1.   Special agency is created when an agent is authorized to perform a particular act without the ability to bind the principal.

      a.   Seller contracts with a broker to find a ready, willing and able buyer.

      b.   Buyer contracts with a broker to locate property.

2.   General agency is created when an agent is authorized to perform a series of acts associated with the continued operation of a particular business (e.g., a property manager employed by a property owner).

3.   Power of attorney gives someone the right to act in place of another as an attorney-in-fact.

F.   Creation of Agency

1.   Actual agency/express agency

      a.   Created through an oral or written agreement

      b.   Agency by subsequent ratification –

2.   Ostensible agency / Authority by Estoppel

      a.   Created when a third party is led to believe an agency relationship exists

      b.   Implied by the actions of the parties

3.   Compensation is not a requirement of an agency relationship. Who pays the agent does not determine whom the agent represents.

G.   **Single Agency vs. Dual Agency**

1.   A single agent represents only one party in a transaction (i.e. – either the seller or the buyer).

2.   Dual agency is when a broker is an agent for both the seller and buyer. Dual agency may arise when a real estate agent shows a property listed with his or her broker to a buyer represented by the same broker. The broker is the dual agent.

3.   Dual agent must keep certain information confidential, unless one principal gives agent written permission to disclose it to the other principal.

a.

b.

c.

4.   All other material information must be disclosed to the other party.

5.   A dual agent must have written consent of both parties.

6.

H.   **Agency Disclosure Law: DISCLOSE – ELECT – CONFIRM**

1.   Licensees are required to provide an agency disclosure form to both parties as soon as practical.

2.   Required in residential transactions involving one to four dwelling units.

3.   Disclosure form is not a contract; it does not create an agency relationship with the consumer.

4.   Agents **"disclose"** on the form the various kinds of agency relationships that can exist in a real estate transaction.

5.   Agents **"elect"** whom they are representing in the specific transaction.

6.   Parties **"confirm"** whom they have elected to represent in the specific transaction in a separate written confirmation in the sales agreement.

I.   Additional Disclosure Obligations

1.   Easton vs. Strassburger decision requires licensees to disclose what they know and what they should know.

        a.   Requires licensee to conduct a visual inspection of accessible areas

        b.   Do not need to inspect common areas of a condominium

2.   Deposits in the form of promissory notes or post-dated checks may be taken, but facts **must be fully disclosed** to the seller.

3.   Must disclose that commissions are negotiable in listing agreements on one-to-four family dwelling units

II.   AGENCY AGREEMENTS

A.   The Listing Agreement

An employment contract that appoints a broker as an owner's special agent, for the specific purpose of finding a buyer who is ready, willing, and able to buy according to the terms of the contract.

1.   Parties

   a.

   b.

2.   Essential elements of a listing agreement

   a.   In writing

   b.

   c.   Amount and/or method of compensation

   - Percentage of gross selling price

   - Flat fee/hourly fee

   d.   "Negotiable commission" clause

   -

   - Price-fixing violates the

   - Can not use listing forms in which the rate of commission is

   e.   Dual agency disclosure and consent provision

   f.   Exclusive types of agreements must contain a definite beginning and termination date.

   g.   Safety clause/protection clause

   - Broker is entitled to commission if prospect buys after listing expires.

   - Broker must give seller a written list of prospects introduced to the property within 72 hours after listing expires.

B.   **Types of Listing Agreements**

1.   Exclusive right to sell

   a.   Agent is paid, regardless of who obtains the buyer.

   b.   A bilateral agreement

   c.   Gives maximum broker protection

2.   Exclusive agency

   a.   Owner retains right to sell himself without paying a commission.

   b.   If anyone other than the owner obtains the buyer, agent gets paid.

   c.   A bilateral agreement

3.   Open/non-exclusive

   a.   Owner may list with more than one broker.

   b.   Listing broker is paid only if he or she obtains buyer, causing possible procuring cause disagreements.

   c.   Unilateral – may be terminated at any time prior to performance.

4.   Net listing

   a.   Broker receives as commission all money above a minimum guaranteed sales price.

   b.   Legal but discouraged in California; broker must reveal amount of expected commission before seller enters into purchase contract.

5.   Option listing

   a.   Used when the broker may want to purchase the property

   b.   Broker must reveal expected profit.

C.   **Buyer Representation Agreement**

1.   Parties

   a.

   b.   Agent (Fiduciary)

2.   Same elements as listing agreement

D.   **Property Management Agreement**

A contract between the owner of an income-producing property and a brokerage that will manage the property

1.   Parties

a.

b.   Broker is agent.

2.   Manager's responsibilities in the agreement are financial, physical and administrative management including:

a.   Marketing space to attract tenants

b.   Collecting rents and complying with rent control rules

c.   Negotiating leases, including investigating applicants' qualifications

d.   Developing a budget and preparing financial reports, including reserves for replacement of short-life items such as air conditioners, appliances, carpeting, etc.

3.   Manager is responsible for performing four types of ongoing maintenance of the property.

a.

b.

c.

d.

4.   In California, every building with 16 or more dwelling units must have a resident apartment manager.

E.   **Termination of Agency Agreements**

- Death or bankruptcy of principal or broker (not salesperson)

- Destruction of improvements

- Performance or expiration

- Mutual rescission

III.   COMMISSIONS

A.   **Broker**

1.   The broker of record is the only one able to receive compensation for real estate services performed.

2.   A broker may receive compensation from anyone including a broker in another state.

3.   Commissions are always fully negotiable and are established by the agreement of the parties, except in two instances:

a.   In probate sales, commissions are established by the probate court.

b.   Under Article 7 of the Real Estate Law, commissions, fees, and costs for certain specified loans are limited by law.

4.   When suing for commission, a licensee must prove that he or she was licensed at the time the act was performed.

B.   **Salesperson**

1.   Salesperson licensees may only receive compensation from their employing broker for activities that require a license.

2.   A salesperson is only permitted to sue his or her broker for a commission, because brokerage contracts are always between the broker and the owner.

C.   **Commission Calculations**

%	x	Paid	=	Made
.06	x	$100,000	=	?
.06	x	?	=	$6,000
?	x	$100,000	=	$6,000

IV. BROKERAGE

A. Broker Responsibilities

To protect against civil claims of malpractice, most brokers will purchase errors and omissions (E & O) insurance. The following are standards required by law.

1. Supervise salespeople and employees (total responsibility).

2. Maintain trust account records.

3.

4. Retain copies of all listings, contracts, cancelled checks, and trust account records.

B. Desk Fee

To determine the "desk fee" – how much it costs the broker to have a salesperson in the office – divide the total office expenses by the total number of salespersons (not the number of desks) in the office.

V.   TRUST FUNDS AND RECORD KEEPING

A.   Trust Funds

1.   Money or things of value

   a.   Received by the broker or salesperson on behalf of another

   b.   In performance of acts for which a real estate license is required

   c.   Held for the benefit of others

2.

3.

   a.

   b.   Failure to place trust funds within three business days into <u>one</u> of the following (unless licensee has buyer/seller written authorization):

   o   A neutral escrow depository

   o   The hands of the principal for whom it was collected

   o   The broker's trust fund account (depositing with broker's personal funds would constitute commingling)

4.

   •

   •   The unlawful taking of another's money

B.   Trust Fund Record Keeping

1.   Record must be kept of all trust funds that pass through the broker's hands.

   a.   No record is required if the funds are **not** touched by the hands of anyone in the broker's office.

   o   Buyer deposits money directly into escrow.

   o   Buyer gives money directly to seller.

   b.   Lack of accounting for trust funds is a serious violation of law even if it is unintentional.

2.   Broker must retain trust fund records:

     a.

     b.   Even if broker does not maintain a trust account at a bank

C.   Trust Account

A demand account (checking) which is identified as a "trust account" and which names the broker as trustee

     a.

     b.   Must provide for withdrawals without prior notice

     c.   Broker may designate one of the following, in writing, to withdraw funds:

         o   Licensed salesperson

         o   Unlicensed individual (e.g. a bookkeeper) must be bonded.

Trust account record must balance.

     a.   Broker must do a

     b.   Deposits should not be returned until buyer's check has cleared.

     c.   Earned commissions should be transferred from the trust account to broker's personal account within no more than 30 days.

     d.   Broker may cover bank service charges by depositing up to

     e.   Commissions: Fees earned by the broker and collectible from trust funds cannot be left in the account for more than 25 days from the date they were earned.

VI.   MORTGAGE LOAN BROKERS

A.   Article 5 of the Real Estate Law

Regulates real estate licensees who broker loans

    a.   Must have written authorization from lender or borrower

- before acceptance of purchase or loan funds,
- to service promissory notes or contracts of sale.

    b.   Broker shall cause the security instrument (mortgage or trust deed) to be recorded prior to disbursing funds, unless the security instrument is delivered to the lender within 10 days following disbursement with a written recommendation to record.

B.   Article 7 of the Real Estate Law (commonly, the "Real Property Loan Law")

1.   Requires a Mortgage Loan Disclosure Statement on all loans negotiated by licensees for 1 to 4-family residential transactions

    a.   On a form approved by the Real Estate Commissioner

    b.   Must be signed by both borrower and licensee and be delivered to the borrower before he or she becomes obligated

    c.   Copy must be retained by broker for three years.

    d.   Disclosure requirements do not apply if lender is an institution such as a bank or S & L, and broker receives a commission not in excess of 2%.

2.   Broker must disclose when lending his or her own funds (or funds of relative of broker).

3.   Maximum commissions are based on type, amount and term of loan.

First loans of less than $30,000

- Under 3 years – 5%
- Over 3 years – 10%

Junior loans of less than $20,000

- Under 2 years – 5%
- Over 2 years but under 3 – 10%
- Over 3 years – 15%

4.   Maximum charges to lendee (not to exceed actual costs)

Based on Loan Amount	Maximum charges
Up to $7800	$390 or actual costs, whichever is less
$7801 to $14,000	5% of loan or actual costs, whichever is less
More than $14,000	$700 or actual costs, whichever is less

5.   **Balloon payments**

      a.   A balloon payment is defined as any payment greater than twice the amount of the smallest payment in the loan schedule.

      b.   Balloon payments are not allowed on loans subject to Article 7 of the Real Estate Law <u>if</u>:

          o   the loan is for less than three years, or

          o   the loan is on an owner-occupied dwelling for a term of six years or less

      c.   No interest only loans in the above situations

      d.   These provisions do not apply to notes from buyers to sellers.

C.   **Usury**

1.   Defined as the charging of an exorbitant amount or rate of interest

2.   Loans made or arranged by a real estate broker secured by real estate are exempt.

VII. FRANCHISE INVESTMENT LAW

A **franchise** is an agreement between two or more persons by which:

- The franchisee is authorized to sell goods and /or services under a marketing plan prescribed by the franchisor, and

- The franchisee's business is associated with the trademark, trade name, logo and advertising of the franchisor, and

- The franchisee is required to pay a franchise fee.

Real estate licensees are authorized to negotiate the sale of a franchise.

VIII. FAIR HOUSING LAWS

A. Civil Rights Act of 1866

Prohibits discrimination based on *race.*

B. Federal Fair Housing Act / Civil Rights Act of 1968

1. Protected classifications:

Race

Religion

Color

Sex

National origin

Familial status

Handicap/Disability

2.   Prohibitions

It is a violation of the Federal Fair Housing Act to do any of the following:

a.   Refuse to show, rent, sell, negotiate, or deal (If asked by seller or buyer to discriminate, broker should cancel listing.)

b.   Offer different terms

c.   Advertise limited availability

d.   Make false statements regarding availability in order to change or maintain the ethnic character of a neighborhood (for example, directing a couple of mixed race to a different neighborhood)

e.   Induce panic selling; (for example, suggesting neighbors should sell because members of a certain racial or ethnic background have moved in)

f.   Deny or alter terms or availability of credit; e.g., refusing to give loans in a particular neighborhood because of the ethnic composition of its residents

3.   Exemptions

a.   The following exemptions never apply when a broker's services are used.

b.   It is not unlawful to discriminate based on religion, color, sex, national origin, familial status, or handicap/disability in the following situations:

- Rental or sale of a single-family home by an owner

- Rental of units (in building with 4 units or less) if the owner occupies one of the units

- Nonprofit organizations may restrict lodgings to members only.

- Rental or sale of units based on familial status involving buildings with at least 80% of the units occupied by someone aged 55 or older.

4.   Complaints must be filed with HUD

- In an administrative hearing, HUD attorneys litigate on behalf of the victim.

- Penalties for violations may include injunctions, damages, court costs, attorney's fees, and civil penalties.

5.   Brokers must display "Equal Opportunity" poster

- Poster must be in each office or place of business

- Failure to display can shift burden of proof to broker in an alleged discrimination complaint.

C.   Equal Credit Opportunity Act (ECOA)

1.   Prohibits discrimination in all consumer credit transactions.

2.   Protected classes are: race, religion, color, sex, national origin, marital status, age and public assistance.

D.   Americans with Disabilities Act (ADA)

1.   Intended to ensure equal access to public accommodations for disabled persons.

- Public accommodations are places accessible to the public (such as businesses).

- Housing accommodations are where people live (covered under Fair Housing Laws).

2.   Prohibits employment discrimination if 15+ employees.

3.   Requires removal of architectural and communication barriers and provision of auxiliary aids and services, if "readily achievable."

4.   New commercial construction must be accessible to the disabled.

5.   Disabled residential tenants may make modifications at their expense. Must return property to original condition.

6.   Those that currently abuse illegal drugs are not considered handicapped or disabled. However, if a person is a recovering alcoholic or AIDS or has HIV/Aids they are considered handicapped or disabled.

E. **California Laws and Regulations**

    1. **Holden Act**

        Prohibits discriminatory lending practices, including **"redlining."**

    2. **Rumford Act**

        a. Prohibits discrimination in the sale, rental, lease, or financing of housing

        b. Declares discrimination in all housing accommodations to be against public policy and is prevented by the exercise of police power

    3. **Unruh Civil Rights Act**

        Prohibits discrimination in accommodations and business establishments

Unit 7: Glossary Review

conversion
principal
agent
exclusive right to sell
exclusive agency
open
dual agency
Americans with Disabilities Act (ADA)

negotiable
fiduciary
blind advertising
commingling
blockbusting
redlining
compensation

1.   One who employs an agent to act on his or her behalf is a _____.

2.   The person employed by a principal to act on his or her behalf is called an _____.

3.   Commissions charged by brokers for their services are fully _____.

4.   A listing agreement in which the owner agrees to pay the agent a commission regardless of who sells the property during the listing period is known as an _____ listing.

5.   A listing which appoints one broker as the sole agent for the sale of a property, but allows the owner to sell it himself without paying a commission is an _____ listing.

6.   A listing that allows an owner to list concurrently with more than one broker is known as an _____ listing.

7.   The relationship of a broker to his or her principal is known as a _____ relationship.

8.   When a broker acts as agent for both the buyer and the seller, it is known as a _____ _____.

9.   _____ is not required to have an agency relationship.

10.   Depositing a client's money in the same account with the broker's personal funds is called _____.

11.   Using trust funds to pay for a broker's personal expenses is called _____.

12.   The illegal practice of inducing panic selling in a neighborhood for financial gain is known as _____.

13.   _____ is the illegal lending practice of refusing to make loans in a particular geographical area based on the location of the property.

14.   The _____ is the federal law that requires buildings to be accessible.

Unit 7: Review Exam

1. A listing broker is the:
    (a)   seller's agent.
    (b)   buyer's principal.
    (c)   seller's subagent.
    (d)   third party.

2. In an exclusive right to sell listing, the principal contracts:
    (a)   with several brokers, each of whom deals with only one third party.
    (b)   to pay the broker a commission regardless of who procures the buyer.
    (c)   with only one broker, but reserves the right to sell the property him or herself without paying a commission.
    (d)   with several brokers.

3. All of the following will terminate a listing without liability **EXCEPT**:
    (a)   destruction of the property
    (b)   mutual agreement
    (c)   expiration
    (d)   the seller has a change of heart

4. If the seller agrees to allow the broker to keep all money received above a certain predetermined amount as his or her commission, what kind of listing do they have?
    (a)   Open
    (b)   Net
    (c)   Multiple
    (d)   Exclusive

5. If a potential client insists that she will not sell her house to members of a certain ethnic group, the broker should:
    (a)   obey her request, in accordance with the law of agency.
    (b)   report the seller to the police.
    (c)   refer her to a fellow salesperson who will obey the request.
    (d)   refuse the listing.

6. Attempting to obtain listings in neighborhoods that are undergoing a change in racial or ethnic composition by playing on the fears and prejudices of owners is known as:
    a)   steering
    b)   commingling
    c)   redlining
    d)   blockbusting

7. The amount of commission paid to a broker is established by:
    (a)   state law
    (b)   negotiation between the broker and the seller
    (c)   local custom
    (d)   real estate boards

8.   A listing in which the principal agrees to contract with only one broker but reserves the right to
     sell the property him or herself without paying a commission is:
     (a)   an exclusive agency listing.
     (b)   an open listing.
     (c)   an exclusive right to sell listing.
     (d)   a net listing.

9.   The listing broker is entitled to a commission according to the terms of an exclusive agency
     listing if the property is sold by any of the following **EXCEPT**:
     (a)   a salesperson employed by the listing broker
     (b)   a salesperson employed by a cooperating broker
     (c)   the listing broker
     (d)   the owner

10. The owner of a property has signed an exclusive right to sell listing contract. Which of the
     following is true?
     (a)   The owner has promised to accept a reasonable offer.
     (b)   The owner has promised to accept any offer identical to the listed price and terms.
     (c)   The owner has promised to pay a commission if the property is sold during the listing
           period.
     (d)   The broker has promised to find a buyer.

11. The clause in a listing agreement that protects the broker's commission if someone with whom
     the broker negotiated purchases the property after the expiration of the listing is known as:
     (a)   a protection clause.
     (b)   a holdover clause.
     (c)   a due-on-sale clause.
     (d)   an override clause.

12. Which of the following establishes the broker's power to act as an agent for the seller?
     (a)   Real estate commissioner
     (b)   Multiple listing service
     (c)   Listing agreement
     (d)   Real estate license

13. An owner unilaterally cancels a 90-day exclusive agency listing after 30 days and then sells the
     property through another broker on an open listing. The seller most probably:
     (a)   owes both brokers a commission.
     (b)   only has to pay the broker on the exclusive agency listing.
     (c)   only has to pay the broker on the open listing.
     (d)   doesn't have to pay any commission.

14. A builder who agrees to pay a commission to the first broker who negotiates a sale would sign:
     (a)   an open listing agreement.
     (b)   a multiple listing agreement.
     (c)   an option listing agreement.
     (d)   an implied listing agreement.

15. If a broker and a seller have a fiduciary relationship, the broker could:
    (a)   inform a buyer that the seller will accept substantially less than the listed price.
    (b)   fail to tell the buyer about hidden structural problems in order to protect the seller.
    (c)   disclose the buyer's financial qualifications.
    (d)   honor the seller's request to refuse to show the property to minorities

16. Which of the following is not required in a listing agreement?
    (a)   Negotiable commission clause
    (b)   Expiration date
    (c)   Listing price
    (d)   Estimated closing costs

17. When a lender refuses to make loans in a given neighborhood because most of its residents are members of a racial minority group, it is an example of:
    (a)   steering
    (b)   blockbusting
    (c)   credit deviation
    (d)   redlining

18. Which of the following would be considered discrimination when advertising the sale or rental of a single family residence?
    a)   "Retiree's dream home"
    b)   "Quiet neighborhood"
    c)   "Female roommate wanted"
    d)   "Apartment complex with chapel"

19. A broker is allowed to maintain personal funds in a trust account so long as the:
    (a)   personal funds do not exceed $500.
    (b)   personal funds are commingled with trust funds.
    (c)   amount does not exceed $200, to cover service charges.
    (d)   interest earned on the personal funds is paid to the broker who maintains the trust account.

20. The Equal Credit Opportunity Act (ECOA) protects borrowers from discrimination based upon the borrower's:
    a)   income
    b)   age
    c)   credit worthiness
    d)   payment record

21. A salesperson has taken a listing in a neighborhood occupied predominantly by Spanish-speaking people. The salesperson decided to advertise the property for sale in a Spanish newspaper that serves the area. To comply with Fair Housing laws, the salesperson should:
    (a)   continue to advertise exclusively in Spanish newspapers.
    (b)   show the property exclusively to Spanish-speaking prospective purchasers.
    (c)   direct English-speaking prospective purchasers away from this property
    (d)   advertise also in one or more English newspapers.

150

Unit 7: Review Exam Key

1. **(a)** The listing broker is the agent for the seller.

2. **(b)** Under an exclusive right to sell listing, the broker is paid regardless of who procured the buyer.

3. **(d)** One party's change of heart does not terminate a listing without liability, unless the other party is also willing to terminate it. The seller would still owe the broker a commission if the terms of the listing were fulfilled.

4. **(b)** For a net listing, price minus net equals commission.

5. **(d)** The broker must not discriminate.

6. **(d)** Blockbusting (panic selling) is the prohibited practice of inducing property sales by representing that bad things will result from an influx of residents of a certain race, religion, color, or national origin, or with some form of disability.

7. **(b)** Commissions are determined by negotiation.

8. **(a)** Under an exclusive agency listing, the owner retains the right to sell the property on his or her own without compensating the listing broker.

9. **(d)** The owner may sell the property without paying a commission in an exclusive agency listing. If anyone else sells the property, the listing broker is entitled to be paid.

10. **(c)** In an exclusive right to sell listing, the broker is entitled to be paid if the property is sold during the listing period, regardless of who obtains the buyer.

11. **(a)** The protection clause protects the broker's commission for a specified amount of time after the listing terminates.

12. **(c)** The listing agreement is a contract by which the seller authorizes the broker to use his or her best efforts to find a ready, willing, and able buyer.

13. **(a)** The seller will probably be obligated to pay both brokers a commission.

14. **(a)** In an open listing, the owner agrees to pay the first broker who negotiates a sale.

15. **(c)** As a fiduciary of the seller, the broker has the duties of loyalty, confidentiality, disclosure, obedience, reasonable care and skill, and accountability. However, these fiduciary duties do not require or permit the broker to commit fraud or violate anti-discrimination laws.

16. **(d)** Closing costs must be estimated upon presentation of an offer, not in the listing agreement.

17. **(d)** Redlining is the prohibited practice of refusing to make loans in certain neighborhoods because of the race or ethnic background of the residents.

18. **(a)** According to HUD guidelines, only choice (a) would constitute discrimination.

19. **(c)** The broker may keep up to $200 in personal funds in the trust account to cover service charges.

20. **(b)** ECOA protects against discrimination based upon the borrower's race, religion, color, sex, national origin, marital status, or age.

21. **(d)** Discriminatory advertising includes practices that indicate a preference that would discriminate.

Unit 8: License Law and Design and Construction

Lecture Outline and Notes

Key topics in this unit:

- Licensing legislation and rules
- Business opportunities brokerage
- Residential design and construction

Reading assignments (in <u>California Real Estate Principles, 6th Edition</u> textbook)

- Chapter 16: The Business of Real Estate
- Chapter 17: Residential Design and Construction

I. **CALIFORNIA REAL ESTATE LAW**

    A. **Found in the Business and Professions Code**

        1. Enacted in 1919

        2. Nation's first licensing law

        3. Recognized need to protect the public from unscrupulous sellers and their agents

        4. Established the Department of Real Estate

            - A department in the

    B. **The Real Estate Commissioner**

        1. Appointed by the Governor

        2. Assisted by the staff of the Department of Real Estate

        3. Determines administrative policy

            - Adopts, amends and repeals regulations that have

4.   Regulates licensees

     a.

     b.   Holds formal hearings under provisions of the Administrative Procedures Act to deny, suspend or revoke real estate licenses

          i.   License revoked – taken away permanently

          ii.   License suspended – taken away temporarily

          iii.   Restricted license may limit term or activities

          iv.

          v.   The real estate commissioner never gets involved in

5.   Enforces the Real Estate Law

     •   Issues brokers licenses, salesperson licenses, PRLS (Prepaid Rental Listing Service) licenses and restricted licenses

6.   Regulates new subdivisions under the Subdivided Lands Law

C.   Commissioner's Advisors

1.   Real Estate Advisory Commission

     a.

     b.

     c.   Meets four times a year in Sacramento, San Francisco, Los Angeles and San Diego

     d.   Makes recommendations and suggestions of policy to the Commissioner

2.   The Attorney General of California is the Commissioner's legal advisor.

3.   in the county in which a violation occurs prosecutes any alleged criminal violations.

D.   Real Estate Education and Research Fund

    1.   20% of all license fees collected by the Commissioner go into this fund, a portion of which is used for education and research projects involving real estate.

    2.   Recovery Account
Parties who have obtained a judgment against a licensed broker that is uncollectible may seek relief from the Commissioner through this fund.

        a.   License is suspended until the licensee makes payment back to the fund.

        b.

        c.

II.   LICENSE LAW

A.   A real estate broker licensee is a natural person or a legal person who, for another person and for a fee:

- Lists, sells, exchanges, manages, buys, rents, arranges loans, negotiates options on real estate; or a business opportunity, or mobile homes previously registered (used) with the Department of Housing and Community Development (HCD).

- The fine for acting as a licensee without a license is

- The Department of Real Estate will not issue or renew a 4-year license of a person who has not paid child support. It may issue a 150-day license, which will automatically be suspended unless evidence is provided that the child support has been paid.

B.   Exceptions

    1.   Anyone dealing with one's own property, unless he or she is in the business of buying and selling real estate paper

    A person is deemed to be "in the business," and is required to have a real estate license, when they sell, buy, or exchange:

        a.   or real property sales contracts (called real estate paper)

        b.

    2.   A corporation dealing with its own property through its regular officers provided they receive no special compensation

    3.   Anyone holding a duly executed power-of-attorney

4.

5.   Court appointed persons (trustees, executors, etc.)

6.   Any assistant, secretary, receptionist, or hostess, provided that person does not quote or discuss prices or terms

- An unlicensed assistant may put together information for an ad, but the licensee must approve it.

- **Note**: If an unlicensed assistant solicits clients, both the assistant and the licensee are liable.

7.   Banks, savings & loans, escrow companies etc., and their employees.

C.   Partnerships

1.   A broker can be a partner with another broker, or

2.   A salesperson subject to the supervision of the broker partner, or

3.   A non-licensee, provided the non-licensee does not perform any acts for which a license is required

D.   Corporate Broker's License

1.   License is issued in the name of the corporation

2.   Must identify a person who holds a broker's license as the designated broker-officer of the corporation

E.   Duty to review

The broker of record has a duty to review, oversee, inspect and manage documents that may have a material affect upon the rights or obligations of a party to the transaction. The broker may delegate this authority to:

1.   Another broker who has written authority

2.   A salesperson who has written authority and two years recent full-time experience

F.   Operating under a fictitious business name (DBA – "doing business as")

Must file a fictitious business name statement with County Clerk

1.   Must renew every five years

2.   Must provide Department of Real Estate with a copy of the DBA filing

G.   Prepaid Rental Listing Service License

A PRLS company is in the business of supplying prospective tenants with listings of residential real properties and charging customers advance fees for their lists.

1.   May be operated by either a real estate broker or a designated PRLS agent

2.   PRLS agents operate under a two-year license issued by the Real Estate Commissioner

H.   A Salesperson Licensee

A person who is employed by a broker, for a fee, to perform any of the acts the employing broker may perform

1.

2.   Regulations of the Real Estate commissioner require a salesperson to have a

3.   A broker licensee can agree to work for another broker in the capacity of a salesperson and must have a written employment agreement and be supervised.

4.   Salespersons and brokers working for another broker are referred to as "associate licensees."

III.   LICENSING REQUIREMENTS

A.   Real Estate Salesperson's License

1.   Education requirement

- One 3 semester unit college level course – Real Estate Principles

2.   Experience requirement

- None

3   After passing the license exam, a person has one year to apply for a license.

4.   All real estate salesperson licenses are issued for four-year terms.

5.

- Must complete, within 18 months:

  a.   a three-semester unit college level course in Real Estate Practice, and

  b.   one additional 3-semester unit college level course

- If condition is not met within 18 months, licensee cannot perform any acts for which a license is required (license is said to be cancelled). However,

  Licensee has until end of four-year license term to complete requirements and remove condition.

- A licensee who does not complete the two-course education requirements by the end of the four-year license term:

  a.   loses his or her license, and

  b.   must take the exam again.

6.   Continuing education requirement

    a.   First renewal of salesperson's license by end of four-year term

            including three hours in each of the following:

- Agency
- Ethics
- Trust funds
- Fair housing

    b.   Subsequent renewals of salesperson licenses require completion of:

            45 hours of continuing education including a minimum of:

- 6 hours in a survey course covering Agency, Ethics, Trust Funds, and Fair Housing

- 18 hours in Consumer Protection designated courses

- 21 additional hours

    c.   If continuing education requirement is not met by end of four-year license term, the license is cancelled, and:

- Licensee has a two-year "grace period" to complete CE requirement, pay late fee and renew license.

- Licensee cannot perform any acts for which a license is required (including receiving compensation for licensed acts) until continuing education is completed and license is renewed.

B. **Real Estate Broker's License**

1.   Education requirements:

- Five are mandatory
- Three are electives
- May be eligible to obtain credit for previous college classes

2.   Experience requirements:

- Two years of experience in a real estate related profession,

  or

- One year experience in a real estate related profession with a 2-year college degree (A.A),

  or

- A 4-year college degree

3.   All real estate broker licenses are issued for four-year terms.

4.   Renewal of broker's license requires completion of 45 hours of continuing education.

C. **License Cancellation**

1.   In the event of death, suspension, revocation or expiration of a broker's license, the active status of all his or her salespersons are cancelled

2.   Cancellation is temporary. Not the same as revocation or loss of license. It means the licensee cannot perform any acts for which a license is required.

3.   If a licensee quits or is terminated, his or her license is cancelled.

- Broker must notify Real Estate Commissioner within ten days using a transfer notice form.
- If a licensee is fired for cause, a notice along with a certified written statement of facts must be sent to the Commissioner.

D. **Common Violations of Real Estate Law**

1. Knowingly misrepresenting value of property to get a listing or secure a buyer.

2. False promise

3. Commingling

4. Secret profit

5. Obtaining license by fraud

6. Convictions involving fraud

7. False advertising

8. Non-member using Realtor® designation

9. Using position of government trust to gain access to confidential records

10. –
   Unscrupulous activity by real estate agents to induce panic selling of homes at prices below market value, by exploiting the prejudices of property owners

11. Discharging a salesperson without notifying the Real Estate Commissioner

12. Undisclosed dual agency

13. Hidden relationships

14. –
   failing to name an agent or to reveal that an agent is involved

15. Failing to notify parties of sales price within one month if no escrow

16. Payment to unlicensed persons

IV. BUSINESS OPPORTUNITY BROKERAGE

A. Definitions

1. A business opportunity is the sale of any type of existing business or enterprise including its goodwill, which is the anticipated continued patronage of a business.

2. If a sale or the lease of the real property of the business is involved, a real estate license is required for people acting in a brokerage capacity.

3. The following documents are used to transfer interests in property in a business opportunity transaction:

    Assignment of lease – if real property is leased

    Deed – if real property is owned

    Bill of sale – for personal property

4. Listing agreements

    a. If an exclusive listing is used to employ a real estate broker it must have a definite termination date.

    b. Oral listings of a business opportunity are enforceable.

    c. The broker must have written authorization of owner before using a send out slip.

B.   **Uniform Commercial Code (UCC)**

1.   A law that attempts to make commercial transactions uniform throughout the country

2.   Covers sale of personal property and the bulk sale of goods of a business

3.   Division 6 of the UCC – The Bulk Sales Law

     a.   Primarily designed to protect creditors but also protects buyers of businesses

     b.   The buyer of a business may:

         i.   Record a Notice of Intention to Sell at least 12 business days prior to the closing

         ii.   Publish it in a newspaper of general circulation

         iii.   Mail a copy to the tax collector

     c.   A complying buyer avoids

     d.   If buyer does not comply with notice provisions of law:

         i.   Agreement between buyer and seller is considered valid as to buyer and seller

         ii.   Agreement can be voided by creditors.

V.   MOBILE HOMES

A.   Personal property under the jurisdiction of the

B.   Real estate licensees are authorized to assist people to buy and sell mobile homes without obtaining a mobile home Dealer's License from HCD, provided the mobile home:

   1.

   2.   is located in a mobile home park where its use may continue for more than a year, or

   3.   has been permanently installed on a foundation on the owner's lot and has thus become real property.

C.   Licensees must, upon notice that a mobile home is no longer for sale, withdraw advertising within

D.   Licensees must give written notice of transfer of a used mobile home not later than the end of the

VI.   **RESIDENTIAL DESIGN AND CONSTRUCTION**

A.   **Building Construction Standards**

    1.   State Housing Law

        a.   Sets building standards for all housing

            Example: Every single-family home sold in California must have an operable smoke detector.

        b.   Enforced by local building officials

    2.   Local building codes

        a.   Set the minimum building standards for all types of buildings and provides for a systematic regulation of construction of buildings within a municipality established by ordinance or law.

        b.   May be more, but never less stringent than the State Housing Law

        c.   Enforced by local building inspectors

        d.   A builder seeking approval for a different type of construction can request an exception to the Building Code.

    3.   State and local health laws – enforced by local health officer

    4.   Energy standards

        R-Value is an indication of the effectiveness of insulation. A higher R number means better insulation. The "R" refers to resistance to heat flow.

        EER stands for "Energy Efficiency Rating." Normally used when referring to air conditioning and heating equipment. The higher the EER number, the more efficient the equipment is.

        SEER stands for "Seasonal Energy Efficiency Rating." Normally used when referring to central air conditioning. The higher the rating, the more efficient the system is over an entire cooling season.

        BTU stands for "British Thermal Unit." It is used in rating a heating unit.

        HVAC stands for "heating, ventilation, and air conditioning."

B.   Construction Measurements

Unit of Measurement	Dimensions	Used to measure:
Board Foot	12" x 12" x 1" = 144 cubic inches.	lumber
Square Foot	1 foot x 1 foot	a floor area or the outside dimensions of a building
Square Yard	3 feet x 3 feet One square yard = 9 square feet	a quantity of carpet or drapery material
Cubic Yard	3 feet x 3 feet x 3 feet	quantities of earth or concrete

C. **Construction Terminology**

Backfill – soil replaced against a foundation

– Building new housing and businesses in vacant or under-utilized lands within existing urban areas, often as part of a reclamation project

Orientation – the placement of a structure on a lot with regard to its exposure to the sun, prevailing winds, privacy from the street and protection from outside noises

Turnkey project – one in which the builder provides a completed facility ready for move-in

Plans:

a. Elevation plan – shows the exterior sides of a structure after all construction has been completed

b. Floor plan – scale drawing showing all dimensions and placements of doors, windows, partitions, and built-ins

c.

a scale drawing showing the dimensions of footings, piers, and details of subflooring

d. Plot plan – indicates lot dimensions and improvements drawn to scale in proportion to the boundary lines. Also shows walks, driveways, and roof plan.

Footing – the base of a building on which the foundation is placed

Flashing –

Mud sill – treated wood member bolted to foundation

Studs – vertical framework placed wall supports

Joists – parallel wooden beams that support flooring or ceiling loads

a heavy horizontal board set on edge at the point of the roof and to which rafters are attached.

– A wall that supports a part of a building, usually a roof or floor above

– A small structure with one or more sides open, such as a newsstand.

slopes on all four sides

Roof Styles

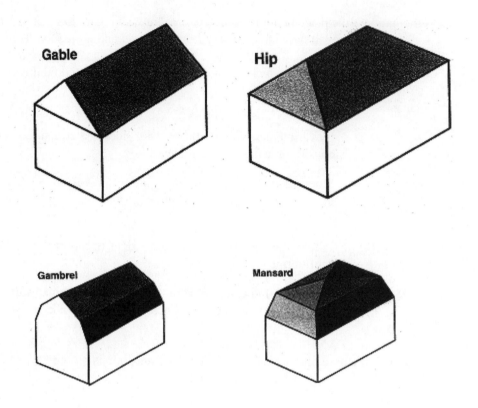

Unit 8: Glossary Review

elevation plan	Attorney General
written	bearing wall
law	floor plan
$10,000	backfill
$20,000	hip roof
turnkey	$100,000
blind advertising	infill

1.   The Real Estate Commissioner's legal advisor is the _____.

2.   A _____ is a load-bearing wall within a building that supports the ceiling joists and upper stories.

3.   The _____ shows the exterior sides of a structure after all construction has been completed. The type and placement of windows are detailed, as are other openings such as doors.

4.   The _____ is a scale drawing showing all dimensions and placement of doors, windows, partitions, and built-ins.

5.   The Real Estate Commissioner investigates verified, _____ complaints against licensees.

6.   The Real Estate Commissioner can adopt regulations that have the force and effect of _____.

7.   A _____ is a pitched roof that slopes on all four sides.

8.   The Recovery Fund allows injured members of the public to collect up to _____ per transaction.

9.   The total amount that can be recovered from the fund per licensee is _____.

10.   The term _____ project refers to a completed construction package ready for occupancy. The last step is to turn over the keys to the buyer.

11.   The fine for acting as a real estate licensee without a license is _____.

12.   _____ is used to replace excavated earth into a hole or against a structure.

13.   Failure to indicate his or her license status in advertising is called

_____.

14.   Building new housing and businesses in vacant or under-utilized lands within existing urban areas, often as part of a reclamation project, is known as _____.

Unit 8: Review Exam

1. A builder submits building plans that the building inspector determines uses some proposed materials that are not in accordance with local building codes. The building inspector determines that the use of these materials would not constitute a safety hazard and approves the plans. This would be an example of:
    (a) An exception
    (b) A nonconforming use
    (c) A variance
    (d) An injunction

2. If local building codes are in conflict with the national Uniform Building Code, which would prevail?
    (a) The local codes always prevail
    (b) The national Uniform Building Code is the highest authority
    (c) The two laws are never in conflict
    (d) The one with the higher standards of health and safety will prevail

3. An unlicensed assistant may give a prospective buyer the address of a listed property, and is also allowed to state:
    (a) What financing terms are available to purchase the property
    (b) The price of the property
    (c) The seller's motivation for selling
    (d) None of the above

4. The maximum amount that may be recovered from the Real Estate Education and Research Fund (Recovery Account) per licensee is:
    (a) 15,000
    (b) 20,000
    (c) There is no limit on the total amount
    (d) $100,000

5. The Real Estate Advisory Commission includes:
    (a) Four broker members and six public members
    (b) Five brokers with five or more years of experience.
    (c) Six broker members and four public members
    (d) Six members from local Boards of Realtors®.

6. Salesperson Johnson has been selling unimproved lots through employing Broker Edwards and receiving a finder's fee from a lender for referring the buyers to the lender. Broker Edwards discovers this and fires Salesperson Johnson and warns all the other salespeople in his office not to be involved in this type of practice. If the Real Estate commissioner finds out about these facts:
    (a) The Commissioner revokes the license of Salesperson Johnson and commends Broker Edwards for firing him.
    (b) Both the broker and the salesperson may be disciplined.
    (c) Broker Edwards could lose his license but in as much as the salesperson has already been fired nothing more can happen to the salesperson.
    (d) The Commissioner fines both the broker and the salesperson.

7.   The period of time a salesperson's license is characterized as being a "conditional license"
      is up to _____ or until two additional college-level courses have been completed.
      (a)   One year
      (b)   18 months
      (c)   Indefinitely, as long as the licensee meets the continuing education requirements.
      (d)   24 months

8.   John and Mary Jackson just purchased a new mobile home one month ago and have decided they
      want to sell it. They contacted Broker Benson to take a listing on it. Broker Benson:
      (a)   Cannot take listings on mobile homes because they are personal property
      (b)   Could not list the mobile home if it had not been registered with the Department of
             Housing and Community Development
      (c)   Could not list the mobile home unless she was also licensed by the Department of Motor
             Vehicles
      (d)   Could not take a listing on a mobile home because it was not installed on a foundation
             and properly registered with the county recorder

9.   Which of the following do not need to have a real estate license when working for another and for
      a fee?
      (a)   Property managers
      (b)   Attorneys doing work incidental to their law practice
      (c)   Loan brokers
      (d)   Brokers specializing in exchanges

10.   The maximum amount that can be recovered from the Recovery Account of the Real Estate Fund
      for damages involving a single judgment is:
      (a) $15,000
      (b) $20,000
      (c)   There is no limit on the total amount involving a single judgment
      (d) $100,000

11.   A real estate license is suspended when the Real Estate Fund pays a judgment creditor of the
      licensee and will not be reinstated until the licensee:
      (a)   Reimburses the judgment creditor plus interest
      (b)   Pays back the Recovery Account with interest
      (c)   Pays back the Real Estate Commissioner plus fines
      (d)   Removes the judgment lien from the public record

12.   The Department of Real Estate will not issue or renew the license of a person who has not paid:
      (a)   Spousal support
      (b)   Traffic fines
      (c)   Child support
      (d)   Real estate board dues

13. A real estate license is not required to buy or sell real estate:
    (a) So long as a person does not do more than 8 transactions a year
    (b) So long as it is a person's own real property.
    (c) So long as a person does not charge more than $10,000 as commission
    (d) So long as a person is acting as an unlicensed assistant under the supervision of a licensee

14. A property is referred to as a "turnkey" project is which of the following?
    (a) A low-income housing project
    (b) A completed project ready for occupancy
    (c) A parcel of land that has all the plans completed
    (d) A condominium project where the keys to the common areas are delivered

15. A piece of metal that is used on a roof to prevent water from seeping through is called:
    (a) Sheathing
    (b) Sole plate
    (c) Flashing
    (d) Soffit

16. A builder needs to use backfill on a project. This would refer to:
    (a) Paving on a roadway
    (b) Gravel used for decorative purposes in landscaping
    (c) Replacing earth against a foundation wall that has been excavated
    (d) Creating a barrier to prevent mudslides

Unit 8: Review Exam Key

1. **(a)**   This is an example of an exception made by a building inspector. The term nonconforming use refers to a use that was at one time acceptable but is no longer allowed. The term variance applies to permission to use land for a purpose that does not strictly conform to a zoning restriction. An injunction is a court order restraining someone from performing a particular action.

2. **(d)**   In this case the higher standard prevails.

3. **(d)**   All of the statements are ones for which a license would be required.

4. **(d)**   The maximum amount that can be paid against one licensee is $100,000. The maximum amount per transaction is $20,000.

5. **(c)**   The Real Estate Advisory Commission consists of six broker members and four public members who are appointed by the Commissioner and who meet four times a year.

6. **(b)**   The broker could be disciplined for not notifying the Commissioner of the violation and the salesperson could be disciplined for receiving commissions from someone other than the employing broker. The Real Estate Commissioner has no authority to fine licensees.

7. **(b)**   A salesperson's license is considered a "conditional license" for up to <u>18 months</u> or until two additional college-level courses (one of which must be Real Estate Practice) have been completed

8. **(b)**   Real estate licensees are not allowed to list mobile homes that are "new" – which means those not registered with the HCD (Department of Housing and Community Development). An exception is allowed if the mobile home is installed on a permanent foundation on an owner's lot.

9. **(b)**   Attorneys do not have to be separately licensed as real estate licensees so long as they are performing acts for which they are licensed as attorneys.

10. **(b)**   The maximum amount that may be recovered from the Real Estate Fund for any one transaction is $20,000. The maximum amount that can be paid against one licensee is $100,000.

11. **(b)**   The Real Estate Law provides that no broker's or salesperson's license suspended under these provisions can be reinstated until the Recovery Account has been repaid, in full, plus interest at the prevailing legal rate.

12. **(c)**   The Department of Real Estate will not issue or renew a license of a person who has not paid child support. In addition, a license will be suspended if a person has not paid child support 150 days following notice.

13. **(b)** A real estate license is not required for buying or selling one's own real property.

14. **(b)** A turnkey project refers to a completed construction package ready for occupancy. The final step is to turn over the keys to the buyer.

15. **(c)** A flashing is a piece of sheet metal (or sometimes composition material) that is used to deflect water from joints or angles, such as roof valleys, or above window and door openings.

16. **(c)** Backfill is used in construction to replace excavated earth into a hole or against a structure.

Notes

Notes

Notes

Notes

Noréd

Notes